WATERFORD
MENNONITE
CHURCH
GOSHEN, INDIANA

COVENANT • BIBLE • STUDIES

Real Families
From Patriarchs to Prime Time

Curtis W. Dubble

faithQuest™ ✦ Brethren Press™

Copyright © 1995 by *faithQuest*. Published by Brethren Press, 1451 Dundee Avenue, Elgin, IL 60120

Brethren Press and *faithQuest* are trademarks of the Church of the Brethren General Board.

All rights reserved. No portion of this book may be reproduced in any form or by any process or technique without the written consent of the publisher, except for brief quotations embodied in critical articles or reviews.

Unless otherwise noted, scripture quotations are from the New Revised Standard Version of the Bible, copyrighted 1989 by the National Council of Churches of Christ in the USA, Division of Education and Ministry.

Cover photo by

99 98 97 96 95   5 4 3 2 1

Library of Congress Cataloging-in-Publication Data

Dubble, Curtis W., 1922-
    Real families : from patriarchs to prime time / Curtis W. Dubble.
       p. cm.— (Covenant Bible study series)
    ISBN 0-87178-735-0 (pbk. : alk. paper)
    1. Family—Biblical teaching. 2. Family—Prayer-books and devotions—English. I. Title. II. Series.
BS680.F3D83 1995
248.4—dc20   94-41676

Manufactured in the United States of America

Contents

Foreword................................. vii
Preface................................... ix
  1. Values and Strengths in Family Life.......... 1
  2. Living as Singles......................... 8
  3. Single-Parent Families 13
  4. Pain and Brokenness in Family Relationships .. 20
  5. Brothers, Sisters, Siblings................. 28
  6. Respecting Boundaries 35
  7. When Parents Fail....................... 42
  8. Passing On Christlike Values to Children...... 49
  9. Changes in Family Life................... 56
10. The Family of God 62
Suggestions for Sharing and Prayer 69

Foreword

The Covenant Bible Study Series was first developed for a denominational program in the Church of the Brethren and the Christian Church (Disciples of Christ). This program, called People of the Covenant, was founded on the concept of relational Bible study and has been adopted by several other denominations and small groups who want to study the Bible in a community rather than alone.

Relational Bible study is marked by certain characteristics, some of which differ from other types of Bible study. For one, it is intended for small groups of people who can meet face-to-face on a regular basis and share frankly with an intimate group.

It is important to remember that relational Bible study is anchored in covenantal history. God covenanted with people in Old Testament history, established a new covenant in Jesus Christ, and covenants with the church today.

Relational Bible study takes seriously a corporate faith. As each person contributes to study, prayer, and work, the group becomes the real body of Christ. Each one's contribution is needed and important. "For just as the body is one and has many members, and all the members of the body, though many, are one body, so it is with Christ.... Now you are the body of Christ and individually members of it" (1 Cor. 12:12, 17).

Relational Bible study helps both individuals and the group to claim the promise of the Spirit and the working of the Spirit. As one person testified, "In our commitment to one another and in our sharing, something happened...We were woven together in love by the master Weaver. It is something that can happen only when two or three or seven are gathered in God's name, and we know the promise of God's presence in our lives."

The symbol for these covenant Bible study groups is the burlap cross. The interwoven threads, the uniqueness of each strand, the unrefined fabric, and the rough texture characterize covenant groups. The people in the groups are unique but interrelated; they are imperfect and unpolished, but loving and supportive.

The shape that these divergent threads create is the cross, the symbol for all Christians of the resurrection and presence with us of Christ our Savior. Like the burlap cross, we are brought together, simple and ordinary, to be sent out again in all directions to be in the world.

For people who choose to use this study in a small group, the following guidelines will help create an atmosphere in which support will grow and faith will deepen.

1. As a small group of learners, we gather around God's word to discern its meaning for today.
2. The words, stories, and admonitions we find in scripture come alive for today, challenging and renewing us.
3. All people are learners and all are leaders.
4. Each person will contribute to the study, sharing the meaning found in the scripture and helping to bring meaning to others.
5. We recognize each other's vulnerability as we share out of our own experience, and in sharing we learn to trust others and to be trustworthy.

Additional suggestions for study and group-building are provided in the "Sharing and Prayer" section. They are intended for use in the hour preceding the Bible study to foster intimacy in the covenant group and relate personal sharing to the Bible study topic.

Welcome to this study. As you search the scriptures, may you also search yourself. May God's voice and guidance and the love and encouragement of brothers and sisters in Christ challenge you to live more fully the abundant life God promises.

Preface

What is a family? Is it parents and children? Is it parents, children, and grandparents? What about live-in aunts and uncles? What about guardians, the church, and the community? There is an African proverb that says it takes a whole village to raise a child. Perhaps a family is every friend, neighbor, relative, and acquaintance in a person's sphere.

In this day, as in Bible times, there are too many ways to configure a family to be able to define family by its members. This look at family has less to do with defining family by "who" and more to do with figuring out "how." How can we be healthy families given the people in our households? How can we trust, respect, love, and appreciate them? How can we communicate better? How can we pick ourselves up from failure and reconcile broken families? What guidance does scripture give us on how to be families?

One time I helped a friend hurriedly plan her 15-year-old daughter's wedding after learning that the girl was going to have a baby. At the church I marveled at the child bride in her borrowed dress made for a fuller, more mature woman and the groom in a sloppy tuxedo, and I wondered, What can these children, hardly more than babies themselves, possibly know about how to be a family?

For that matter, what did I know about families at the ripe old age of twenty-five? Our only real training for family life is experience, and each of us begins gathering experience in family living from the minute we are born. In their short life experience, these two children already knew a lot of things about life and family. They were acquainted with pain, decision-making, sacrifice, and boundaries. But the one thing that would help them survive the difficult years ahead was unconditional love. They loved each other, their parents loved them, and their God loved them. Love alone cannot make a family, but no family will work without it.

May your personal family and your covenant family be strengthened by this study.

Julie Garber
Editor

Recommended Resources:

Anderson, Herbert and Robert Cotton Fite. *Becoming Married*. Westminster John Knox, 1993.

Anderson, Herbert and Susan Johnson. *Regarding Children*. Westminster John Knox, 1994.

Anderson, Herbert and Kenneth R. Mitchell. *Leaving Home*. Westminster John Knox, 1993.

Curran, Delores. *Traits of a Healthy Family*. Harper, San Francisco, 1985.

Friedman, Edwin. *Generation to Generation*. Guilford Press, 1986.

Napier, Augustus and Carl Whitaker. *The Family Crucible*. Bantam, 1984.

Satir, Virginia. *New Peoplemaking*, 2nd ed. Science & Behavior, 1988.

Just Family Nights. Edited by Susan Vogt. Brethren Press, 1994.

1

Values and Strengths in Family Life
Ruth 1:1-18;
Matthew 1:18-25; 2:13-15, 19-23

What are the family values that so many people hold sacred but few can describe? The Bible stories of Ruth and Naomi and Mary and Joseph give us some insight into what family values are and how they are related to Christian faith.

Personal Preparation
1. Read Ruth 1:1-18 and Matthew 1:18-25; 2:13-15, 19-23. How would you describe these two families? Compare your own family experience to these.
2. Think about your family as you were growing up. What family values did your family model for you? How much time did you spend together? How much trust did you have? How well did you communicate?
3. Jot down your weekly family routine. Where in this schedule do you take time to encourage Christian values such as trust, faith, communication, and reconciliation? Find time this week as a family to talk about how your family can give priority to encouraging family values.

Understanding

Everyone seems concerned about family values. Virtually every magazine and newspaper features family values, or the lack of them. Secular and religious bookstores have whole sections devoted to family. And every politician has to mention family values in campaign speeches to be elected. Why all this interest? As a culture, we are moving through waves of rapid transition and crises. People are looking to families for stability, an anchor of civilization in a culture churning like the high seas.

Family values are both a big issue and a fuzzy issue. While family values are fashionable, no one is quite sure what family values are or who has the best ones, or whether family values can truly right our sinking ship.

In his book *A Church Guide for Strengthening Families,* Jim Larson draws from two major family research projects to come up with a list of characteristics of healthy families. He believes that healthy families value . . .

Appreciation. Healthy families appreciate each other and find ways to express that appreciation.

Time. Healthy families work hard to be together even with busy schedules. They make an effort to spend both quality and quantity time in play and togetherness.

Communication. To be strong, families must communicate well. Communication should be direct, loving, and constructive. But communication is not only clear expression. It also requires listening carefully and understanding.

Commitment. A family that wants to work on wholeness must possess a strong will to remain together, even during times of transition, difficulty, or crisis.

Faith. Healthy families seem to share similar moral and spiritual beliefs. They desire to be obedient to the will of God, which, for the family of God, is to be loving, trusting, gracious, respectful, and responsible to each other. The values of Christian faith are the values of the family.

Adaptability. Strong families deal with difficulties and unexpected events in positive and constructive ways. They prefer adaptability over rigidity. They search for alternative ways to resolve conflicts.

That's Not All

For this study I suggest several other qualities that strong families value:

Security. Healthy families want security. They place importance on helping each member feel sure that their physical and emotional needs will be met and that they are loved unconditionally.

Freedom. Healthy families respect the freedom and choices of others. It is appropriate for families to offer plenty of guidance. If they do, they can trust that personal choices will be well informed and that each person knows the consequences of choosing.

Intimacy. Healthy families are physically and emotionally close. They come together to share hopes, failures, successes, thoughts, fears, and joys with each other. Family leaders encourage and model intimate behavior.

Trust. Family members trust that others in the family will carry out responsibilities, give love and support, and provide necessities of food, shelter, and clothing.

These values, promoted in the Bible as Christian family values, make families strong and healthy. While many Bible families failed to embrace God's plan for families, at least two, Naomi's family and Mary and Joseph's new family, exemplify what it means to be a healthy family.

As outsiders looking in on Ruth and Naomi and Mary and Joseph, we catch only a glimpse, one moment out of two family histories that span years. We cannot look to the Bible to see the day-to-day details of who is shirking household duties or keeping secrets or pushing the limits of discipline. But we do see two stories that tell us generally how God means for us to live together as families.

Ruth and Naomi

Naomi and Elimelech had two sons. When famine struck Palestine, Elimelech escaped starvation by fleeing with his family to a land called Moab, east of the Salt Sea. While food was plentiful in Moab, there were some undesirable trade-offs. Moab was antagonistic toward Judah and Judahites; Moabite religious practices did not revere Israel's God; and refugees like Elimelech and his family were considered alien residents without rights of citizenship.

It's hard to imagine things getting worse, but they did. Elimelech died, leaving Naomi a widow. Then the two sons, who had taken Moabite wives, also died. Grieving and discouraged, Naomi was left in an alien land with two daughters-in-law. Without men to earn a livelihood and children to promise a future, the women faced poverty and discrimination.

Because families meant survival in Naomi's time, how would she survive without husband, sons, and grandchildren? Despite the destruction of her traditional family, Naomi and her daughters-in-law became a family, exhibiting almost all the values in our list. Operating under these values, the women eventually made their way out of the crisis.

Following the deaths of the men in the family, Naomi was concerned about the security of the surviving women. With little thought for herself, she planned to release the daughters from any obligation to her and return them to the security of their birth families in Moab. She gave them a blessing—"May the Lord deal kindly with you, as you have dealt with the dead and with me. The Lord grant that you may find security in the house of your husband"(1:8-9)—and she urged them to go.

Naomi gave them options for leaving. One daughter chose to stay in Moab. The other chose to go with Naomi. "When Naomi saw that [Ruth] was determined to go with her, she said no more to her" (1:18). She seemed to respect Ruth's freedom to choose. She had already advised Ruth of the dangers and now needed to accept the young daughter-in-law's decision. This is a difficult family value to hold, especially when family members make choices that are objectionable to parents and siblings. Though she may have disagreed with Ruth's decision, Naomi allowed Ruth to join her.

Then there was a tender moment of intimacy. Orpah departed with a tearful kiss while Ruth clung to her mother-in-law, refusing to leave. Although we often think of intimacy as a sexual activity, family intimacy is much more than that. Intimacy is the degree to which we share our life with someone else, physically, emotionally, and spiritually. These women's lives were intertwined deeply and affectionately. Separation was difficult because so much of their lives was wrapped up in the lives of others.

Ruth exhibited the family value of commitment when she pledged to stay by Naomi, risking her own safety and happiness. Though couples today use Ruth's familiar words to Naomi in weddings (see 1:16-17), they are rarely in a similar dangerous predicament. In contrast, Ruth's loyalty was remarkable when we consider that her pledge to Naomi came at great sacrifice. She was willing to become a foreigner without privilege, face poverty, and leave her own people out of commitment to Naomi. In her pledge, Ruth declared that "your God shall be my God" (1:16). This family of two was bonded by a faith in Naomi's gracious God. And just as God was gracious to them, they were gracious to each other.

Family values figure prominently in this one brief chapter in the small Book of Ruth. This story, however, is far more important than its length would indicate, because it is about the ancestral family of Jesus. Centuries later, Matthew gave us a genealogy that tells us what kind of family Jesus was born into, and there in the long list of names is Ruth. Also listed are Tamar, who tricked her father-in-law into lying with her to produce heirs, and Bathsheba, whose child Solomon was a beloved and brilliant ruler. While we would not approve of all their behavior, Jesus' ancestors represent a strong love of family.

Mary and Joseph

Mary and Joseph, Jesus' most immediate family, also demonstrate strong family values. Like Ruth and Naomi, this young family also started out in a serious predicament. Mary was pregnant before she actually married Joseph, and Joseph claimed the child was not his. Not wanting to bring a death sentence upon her for adultery, Joseph planned to divorce her. But then Joseph was visited by an angel who told him of God's plan for the family. After this visitation, Joseph had a whole new view of his family. Mary already knew of the plan, of course, and joyfully awaited the baby Jesus. Now Joseph, the seemingly "righteous" one, was even more righteous in his wish to please God, so he claimed the child and Mary and they became a family.

In a short and tumultuous time, the newly married couple learned about adaptability, communication, appreciation, and commitment.

Despite all the adversity the family would face, Joseph and Mary were finally committed to facing the adversity together. But the most interesting thing about this family is that, according to Gospel accounts, they discovered what true family life was through a series of encounters with angels and the Holy Spirit. They wanted to be obedient to the will of God, which was, they discovered, for them to become a family for the Messiah. They had to put aside self-interest and embarrassment and embrace each other and the child, promising to raise him for the ministry God would provide. Joseph and Mary provided a link between family and faith.

That was not the end of the crisis for Joseph, Mary, and Jesus. Herod resented the child king and decreed that all boys under two years of age in and near Bethlehem should be killed. Thinking only of Jesus' security, Joseph and Mary fled with the child to Egypt, returning only when the furor was over. Jesus' life began and ended in crisis, but from the first to the last, Mary and Joseph nurtured the child, respected him, trusted him, appreciated him, and believed in him.

Easier Said Than Done

Christian families don't often spring up by decree of the angels, and they don't always succeed under pressure like Ruth and Naomi or Mary, Joseph, and Jesus. But just as God patiently teaches individuals how to walk in faith and love, God has grace for families who are struggling to be healthy. When we berate ourselves for failing as Christian mothers and fathers and children, we often forget to extend God's grace to ourselves.

One such woman is Carole Gossnickle, who frequently berated herself about failing as a Christian mother. Once again she was feeling bad about not living up to her expectations as a Christian. One day, as she tugged away at the weeds in her flower garden, a quiet voice within her said, "What did you do when your children were learning to walk and they fell down?" Carole thought to herself, I picked them up, kissed their hurt, and told them they were okay. The inner voice asked again, "You mean you didn't spank them or scold them because they fell?" Very indignantly Carole thought, of course not! They were just learning and doing the best they could!

Then, very gently and lovingly, the voice within said, "Carole, that is how I feel about you when you fall" (adapted from *The Upper Room*, August/September 1987, p. 42).

No family measures up completely. Fortunate is the family who, with godlike spirit, can lift each other up like infants and surround each other with cords of human kindness. Like God comforting Hosea, we ought to be able to say:

> I took them up in my arms; but they did not know that I healed them. I led them with cords of human kindness, with bands of love....
> I was to them like those who lift infants to their cheeks. I bent down to them and fed them. (Hos. 11:3-4)

Discussion and Action

1. Name the positive family values you see in Naomi's extended family and in Jesus' birth story. Are there other values in *your* household that are not evident in these two biblical stories?
2. Undoubtedly the question will arise, what is family? Consider the variety of shapes and sizes of households today and how your congregation is assisting in strengthening the faith and relationships of such persons.
3. Mothers, fathers, children, grandparents move frequently these days. Some transitions are intentional, some forced. Some, like Elimelech and Naomi, move because of natural disasters (famine); some, like Joseph and Mary, move because of political oppression. Ask each other about the moves you made as families. Why? What held you together or pushed you apart?
4. In the writings of Isaiah 43:1-7 and Hosea 11:1-11, God is revealed as a parent. Talk about God's centrality in your home. Consider how frequently this theme is taught, preached, or emphasized in your congregational life.
5. The religious training of Naomi and her daughters-in-law was different. It is obvious, in the account, that Naomi's faith witness in God proved winsome. How do you teach the value of diversity in your house? Discuss the importance of faith-sharing and faith-living.
6. During the next twenty-four hours, share with a person in your family structure your appreciation for a value or strength that person brings to your family. Share it verbally and physically.

2

Living as Singles
Ruth 1:6-18
1 Corinthians 7:1-9, 32-40

The Bible challenges Christians to include singles in all parts of church life and even holds up singlehood on occasion as the preferred lifestyle. Without obligations to spouse and children, the single person can give the whole self to obedience to God.

Personal Preparation

1. Examine your own attitude toward singleness. Is it good, bad, normal, or superior to other ways of living? Why?
2. Read Ruth 1:1-18. Pay attention to the conversation between Naomi and Ruth in verses 15-18. Is it possible to be truly single? Is it possible to be so united with another that two become one?
3. Read 1 Corinthians 7:1-9, 32-40. Do you think being single relieves people of anxiety about life and allows them to think only of pleasing God? Why or why not?
4. If you are single, what do you like about it? If you are married, what do you envy about the single life?
5. Think of a single person you deeply appreciate. Ask yourself, why? Consider including your reasons in your group discussion.

Understanding

A widow was learning to live alone after years of marriage. She said, "In this country [the United States] people frequently walk in pairs. If you are alone, you are a misfit, an oddball, and sometimes an embarrassment to your married friends. Sometimes persons aren't quite sure how or whether to include me in their activities."

She might have added that some churches still perpetuate the idea that unmarried people are to be pitied, considered unfulfilled, or incomplete. Some Christians still think that singleness is a lusterless, second-class, second-best status.

Social convention and the value we place on marriage may keep people from seeing that scripture presents both marriage and singleness as valid ways of living. At times, remaining single is even directed by God or is seen as the preferred choice. Throughout much of Christian history, people have honored singleness as a vocational choice with a high calling. In this study we will look at biblical characters who were single for one reason or another and whose lives were rich and rewarding. For Jeremiah and Paul, singleness was a calling; for Ruth it was a circumstance that turned into an opportunity. Whatever the reasons for their singleness, their examples demonstrate that every Christian lifestyle has pitfalls and promise. Singleness has its problems, but it is also full of potential that the church must learn to value.

Single by Circumstance

In the beginning Ruth did not choose to be single. She was married and then widowed. Her predicament involved the hard-luck family of Elimelech and Naomi from Bethlehem of Judah (Ruth 1:1-18). Famine drove Naomi, her husband, Elimelech, and their two sons into the land of Moab where the Judahite God was not revered and strangers were without rights. Here, however, they found refuge and sustenance for many years—until another tragedy struck. Elimelech died. Chilion and Mahlon cared for their mother and brought Moabite wives of their own to the family. The women were named Orpah and Ruth. But before the couples produced heirs, the sons died, leaving the women more than grief-stricken. Women alone without husbands or children had no economic means, no prospects for living.

This circumstance happens often in our own culture to spouses, particularly women, both young and old. They may rely on a husband for income, financial management, and household maintenance. Then suddenly one day, the husband dies unexpectedly leaving the woman with great financial needs and very little know-how. If she is elderly, employment may be out of the question. If she is young with children, employment may be impractical. Moreover, children may represent support in the future, but young children are a financial responsibility, complicating life for a single parent.

Such was the predicament for Ruth and Naomi. Naomi did what many singles find themselves doing today, moving back home with relatives. Hearing that the famine in Judah was over, Naomi decided to return to her kin in Bethlehem. She encouraged her daughters-in-law to stay in their homeland and remarry for security. She also relieved them of any responsibility to her as daughters-in-law. Orpah took Naomi's advice, but Ruth refused to leave her mother-in-law. She refused the option of returning home to marry and chose to remain with Naomi instead. She pledged to learn to know Naomi's people and her God and die where Naomi would die.

Ruth rejected marriage, but she did not reject family. Like many childless, single people today, Ruth belonged to a family, an intimate group of people who trusted, shared, respected, and defended each other. The fact that she had no mate did not disqualify her from being a member of a family.

"Single" is a poor label for people who do not have mates or children. Very few people in the world are truly alone. Single people have siblings, parents, nieces, nephews, children, or groups whom they adopt as family, such as church family or groups of close friends.

Single by Choice

Taken another way, singleness may require the rejection of family. The prophet Jeremiah heard a call from God that instructed him to remain single and to reject the attachments of family. Jeremiah said, "The word of the Lord came to me: You shall not take a wife, nor shall you have sons and daughters in this place" (Jer. 16:1-2).

Why would God advise Jeremiah to remain single? God had something for Jeremiah to do that required his full devotion. Jeremiah was assigned the difficult and all-consuming job of preaching God's message and telling the people that, because they were unfaithful, bad things were about to happen. The competition between the duties of his call and the duties of family would make Jeremiah less effective. Moreover, Jeremiah's innocent family would, by association, be scorned by the people who blamed the messenger for the bad news.

Vivid in my memory are the discussions of adults during the 1970s when the arms race was at its height. With a nuclear holocaust hanging over their heads, people felt it was irresponsible to bring children into the world only to suffer. And like Jeremiah, some felt they must devote themselves singlemindedly to working for peace. There was no time for spouses and families. In times of moral upheaval, some people may feel God's call to be single and work for change. In times of danger, some people may feel God's call to refrain from having families in order to spare sons and daughters anguish and pain.

Apostle Paul's writings in 1 Corinthians 7:1-9, 32-40 reflect some of this same thinking. The membership of the Corinthian congregation had written a letter asking for clarity on several issues including singleness and marriage. The entire seventh chapter is dominated by the expectation of the Lord's return. Since the age is to be drawing near to its close and is expected to bring great disorder upon the world, Paul advises that it is far better for believers to be faithful and devoted to God than to be distracted by worries of marriage and family. "I think that, in view of the impending crisis, it is well for you to remain as you are. . . . I mean, brothers and sisters, the appointed time has grown short. . . . For the present form of this world is passing away" (1 Cor. 7:26-31). While Paul never encourages people to abandon their families, he gives preference to the single life and pleasing the Lord.

Paul also felt that a single person committed to Christ could give undivided attention to the work of the Lord in a way that a married person could not. Paul could have been rationalizing his own choice to be single, but we know from this passage that he believed marriage was honorable and divinely ordained. He also rejects any suggestion that marriage is sinful. In the end, however, he is of the definite opinion that singleness is the supreme life for a disciple. He himself remained unmarried so that his devotion to Jesus and God's kingdom would be undivided. "The unmarried man is anxious about affairs of the Lord, how to please the Lord; but the married man is anxious about the affairs of the world, how to please his wife, and his interests are divided" (7:32-34).

Paul makes his case for singleness as a vocation yet respects the matter of choice. "I wish that all were as I myself am. But each has a particular gift from God, one having one kind and another a different kind" (7:7).

As a staff member of the International Fellowship of Evangelical Students, Ada Lum traveled all over the world. In her book *Single and Human*, Ada says, "[F]or a long time I did not consider that my single status was a gift from the Lord. I did not resent it—to be frank, in my earlier idealistic period I thought that because I had chosen singleness I was doing God a favor! But in later years I was severely tested again and again on that choice. Then, through Paul's words and life and my subsequent experiences, it gently dawned on me that God had given me a superb gift! Once this truth took root in me ... I found myself stretching out more eagerly and confidently for life."

Whatever our status—married or single—God has given us a way to be faithful.

Discussion and Action

1. How does your group view singleness? Is it a different way of forming family (Ruth)? a vocation (Paul)? a problem?
2. Talk about your thoughts on preparation question no. 2. What do you like about being single, if you are single. What do you envy about being single, if you are married?
3. Is anyone ever truly single? How do singles achieve deep relationships and intimate friendship?
4. What can single people teach others about friendship, independence, and self-esteem?
5. How do married people develop their individuality aside from their primary partner? Is this easier for singles?
6. Talk about ways your covenant group or congregation can change to make singles feel more welcome. Also, consider ways to challenge singles to think of the single life as a gift. How can singleness be used in your congregation?
7. Think of Jesus' friends. How does marital status fit in? Do we know much about their status? What importance does it play for Jesus?

3

Single-Parent Families
Genesis 21:1-21; Luke 7:11-17

For various reasons, many families today have only one parent living in the home. Families of the Bible were no different. Their reliance on the religious community and on God for material and moral support demonstrates that the centrality of faith in family is more important than the number of parents.

Personal Preparation

1. With an 8.5" x 11" sheet of paper and a box of crayons, draw a picture of your family from your childhood. Indicate by color the influence each parent or guardian had on you. Note any traumatic experiences that affected your family, such as illness, economic hardship, discrimination, or disaster. Bring your drawing to your covenant group and tell about its significance.
2. With imagination read Genesis 21:1-21 and Luke 7:11-17. Also read the earlier story of Hagar's experiences from Genesis 16. Watch how Sarah becomes cruel. How does the story of Hagar and Ishmael make you feel?
3. Identify emotionally with one of the single mothers in these stories and record some of your thoughts.
4. Read Luke 7:11-17. Keep track of any feelings of anger, sadness, or joy that arise as this and the story of Hagar unfold. Write them down.

Understanding

While culture has dictated that two parents are better than one, it is very common these days for one parent to manage a family without a partner. How do men and women become single parents? They have children out of wedlock, a spouse dies, couples divorce, a parent deserts the family, or one parent works in a distant place. Also some people decide at the outset that they want to raise children alone and find ways to create a family on their own.

The Bible doesn't help us know whether single-parent families are good or bad. It only lets us know that single-parent families are a fact of life. But according to the biblical record, God has compassion for even the smallest family, one parent and one child. Despite the hardships of single-parent families, including abandonment, poverty, and overwhelming parental responsibility, all the necessary elements of life and faith can be found there. That is what counts.

Hagar and Ishmael

Hagar was the head of a single-parent family in the Bible. Genesis 16 tells how she came to be the single mother of a son named Ishmael. There we learn that she had little choice about starting a family. She was a victim of cultural circumstances.

Hagar, an Egyptian slave girl, served Abraham's wife, Sarah. As fate would have it, her mistress could not provide her husband with an heir or a future. In that culture barrenness was not only a social disgrace, it meant economic disaster. Children and grandchildren could work and provide for the family. It also meant death, the end of the family line. God had promised Abraham and Sarah heirs, but as they aged, they doubted it would ever happen. And since it was acceptable in that culture for one wife to claim the offspring of her husband and another wife, Sarah sent Abraham to Hagar. She said, "You see that the Lord has prevented me from bearing children; go in to my slave-girl; it may be that I shall obtain children by her" (Gen. 16:2). A child born of such a union was reckoned as the child not of the handmaid, but of the wife, by adoption.

Abraham, becoming impatient as he waited for God's promises to come true, listened to and agreed to the plan. He lay with Hagar and she conceived. The boy who was born, Ishmael, was to be Abraham and Sarah's heir according to custom.

It was an unhappy situation all around. Both Sarah and Hagar were bound by cultural conventions. Sarah believed she must provide an heir, and Hagar was forced into parenthood without any part in the decision. She became a single mother because of the fear, disgrace, and disappointment of her slaveowners. Her pregnancy was prearranged without her welfare being considered. Hagar had contempt for her situation and for Sarah who got her into this mess. And Sarah, who resented the need for another woman to bear her child, "dealt harshly" with Hagar.

After Hagar's child was born, God fulfilled the promise that Sarah would conceive and bear a child. Sarah insisted that her son, Isaac, would be the rightful heir of Abraham's family, not Ishmael. Out of jealousy and anger, she became even more cruel to Hagar. When Sarah saw her son Isaac playing with Ishmael, she shouted to Abraham, "Cast out this slave woman with her son; for the son of this slave woman shall not inherit along with my son Isaac!" (Gen. 21:10).

Abraham rose early in the morning and gave Hagar some bread and water to take with her in her exile. Suddenly she and Ishmael were a single-parent family. The security of their home was gone. They were alone in the wilderness of Beersheba (21:14).

People experience the same thing today. A woman named Monica had been married for fourteen years. She and her husband, Alex, were professional types. Four children enlivened their lives. Church life was a weekly priority. They seemed like an ideal family. But late one night, Alex stunned Monica when he said he wanted out of the relationship. He was no longer happy in the marriage and family. "It felt like a severe earth tremor to me," remarked Monica. For the next several months, each attempt to understand the problem or to work on solutions led to a dead end.

When Alex left the family with no hint of returning, Monica's whole world changed. The weight of suddenly being a single parent of four young children was extremely heavy. "Alex had a choice. I felt like I was a victim of circumstances," exclaimed Monica. Like Hagar, Monica faced the harsh reality of being thrust into the role of managing a family without a partner.

The first thing that Hagar and Monica face as single parents is economic struggle. Statistics show that in the major cities of the United States a high percentage of the homeless are single parents and their children who have fallen on economic hard times. With only one income, a single parent has meager financial resources. Hagar's bread did not last long. Neither does a savings account or the paycheck of one parent. When the water in the skin container was gone, Hagar placed her little Ishmael in the shade of a bush. Walking a distance from him she sat down and cried saying, "Do not let me look on the death of the child" (21:16).

Monica has her economic story too. A single-parent family often means twice as much responsibility, twice as many demands on a parent's time and energy and half the earning power. In her case she was working only two days a week when Alex walked out. There were times, after her four children were tucked lovingly in their beds, that she slumped into the living room chair and cried. Sometimes in desperation she cried, "God, help us! Help us!"

Other problems come with single-parent families. When one parent dies or leaves abruptly, the remaining parent often must find new friends and supporters. Friendships with other couples may disintegrate. When one of the foursome departs, either the couple breaks off the relationship rather than choosing sides in a marital conflict, or the single person in the relationship feels like the odd one out in the newly configured threesome. It is easier and more rewarding to find new friends and one-on-one relationships.

The task of parenting alone is another challenge for the single parent. As the sole disciplinarian, a single parent may feel like he or she is always the family police officer, the killjoy, and the overreacting, uptight adult.

Carrying the sole responsibility, a single parent must look after all the childcare and be the one available at all times to respond to needs and emergencies. A single parent has to be the adult role model for children, not just a gender model. If the single parent wants a model of the other sex for his or her children, he or she has to arrange for that as well. In other words, a single parent must be "on" at all times. There is no one on a day-to-day basis to spell the single parent.

Life is not easy for children in a single-parent family, either. They do not have the luxury of two primary relationships. Everything, good or bad, is wrapped up in one parent. When a child in a single-parent family is able to take on parentlike responsibilities, he or she may have to begin working earlier in life than other children, become a "parent" to younger siblings, and make personal sacrifices for the good of the whole family.

The story of Hagar and Ishmael holds out hope for single families. Despite the story's sorrows, some beautiful details attest to the strength of this single mother and her son. In the midst of crisis, a new understanding of God's presence and care came to

Hagar. Hagar was out of water. She had given up hope that she and Ishmael would survive in the desert. So she surrendered the child to fate, placing him under a bush and turning away before she would have to see her own child die. At this tense moment an angel of God spoke to her (just as God spoke to Abraham at the moment he was to sacrifice Isaac). This messenger said that God would be with her and would make a nation of Ishmael's offspring. "Then God opened her eyes and she saw a well of water . . . and gave the boy a drink" (21:19).

God is a support to single families, someone to give courage and hope. Hagar said to God, "You are Elroi [which means you are a God of seeing or God who sees]; . . . Have I really seen God and remained alive after seeing him?" (16:13). When our backs are figuratively against the wall, God is a true resource to us.

Crises that draw us closer to a reliance on God are a blessing of sorts. Single parenting is full of such crises and stories about reliance on God and the church. From the precarious life of single-parent families, traditional two-parent families stand to learn something about the blessings of a closer relationship with God.

Monica tells how her relationship to the church deepened through her own family crisis. The first Christmas following her husband's departure, an anonymous gift of money was sent to her from some person or people in the congregation where they attended. She exclaimed, "It was God-sent!" For several years similar gifts came through the mail. It's amazing how the God who sees, Elroi, responds then and now to needs of single parents.

The Widow of Nain

Single parents appear in the New Testament, too. Luke 7:11-17 introduces us into the middle of a funeral procession in a town called Nain. The only son of a widow had died, leaving his mother alone in the world. Unlike Hagar, the widow of Nain lost her only means of security, her child.

In Bible times if a man died, his widow often suffered at the hands of the powerful (Job 24:21). Frequently she was exploited by others even though the Jewish law forbade it (Exod. 22:22). The prophet Isaiah spoke out against such social irresponsibility, saying, "Ah, you who make iniquitous decrees . . . that widows may be your spoil, and that you make the orphans your prey" (Isa. 10:1-2).

Widowhood was like being an outcast. This was especially true if she had no family to provide for her. This widow of Nain felt both the pain of her son's death and the accompanying social stigma. Jesus reached out to her with compassion and life.

Without a husband or child, the woman would be a social outcast and a burden on the community. Not only that, she would be all but dead herself. We find life in our relationships with other people. We derive our identity from our family and friends. But this woman was entirely alone until Jesus saw her and her dead son and brought the boy back to life. He blessed them both with life. The boy regained his breath and the mother regained her purpose, her future, and her family.

Jesus' act of compassion does not say anything about which kind of family is best. It says that all families, regardless of their circumstances, are blessed by God. Jesus typically ministers to the lowest of social outcasts to demonstrate that everyone is worthy of being loved. The single-parent family in Bible times was regarded poorly, but Jesus regards the single mother highly.

Our churches can be judgmental about the circumstances of families with no resources and only one parent. They tend to look on people like Hagar and the widow of Nain as freeloaders and burdens. Churches believe that people get themselves into these situations by choice when, in truth, single parenthood is often uncontrollable, as it was for Hagar and the widow. Jesus' blessing for the widow of Nain challenges the church to support families, regardless of the number of parents or the configuration of its members or the family's circumstances.

Single-parent families may show us after all that love, security, mutual up-building, and faith are all the more central in the single-parent family that leans on God than in the traditional two-parent family that has not struggled and come to see the face of God.

Discussion and Action

1. Share the drawing of your family that you prepared for this session, and talk about the different types of families represented in your covenant group.
2. What thoughts and feelings came to you as you read the stories of Hagar and the widow of Nain.
3. Jesus' compassion brought new life into the house of the widow of Nain. Would Jesus have shown the same compassion if the widow had been divorced or if the son was a victim of AIDS? What do you think?

4. At the raising of the widow's son, someone who was there said, "God has looked favorably on his people!" God is gracious toward all. Does this mean it is all right to plan a single-parent family or to divorce and become a single-parent family? What kind of family does God want us to have? Does the Bible tell us?
5. When people lose a spouse by death or divorce, a visit from someone in the congregation during the first or second week after the death or separation is very important. As a single parent, what help would you want from the congregation? As a layperson, what would you say to a single parent in crisis?
6. How does our church and society encourage or discourage prejudice against single-parent families? What form does the prejudice take? Discrimination? Neglect?
7. Are you a child of a single parent? Tell about your experience, if you are able. In your experience, how has the church treated single-parent families?
8. Brainstorm ideas for supporting single-parent families, such as establishing support groups, providing childcare, mentoring children who need role models, and giving financial advice.
9. Have someone bring statistics on poor children in single-parent families in your community. How many children live below the poverty line in your community? How many families have only one parent? What services are there in your community for single-parent families?

4

Pain and Brokenness in Family Relationships
Genesis 29:1—30:30; Mark 7:9-13

Virtually every family experiences pain and brokenness. Families in the Bible knew about ruptured family relationships, too. This session shows what families do under stress and what role the church can play in reconciliation, renewal, comfort, and prevention.

Personal Preparation

1. Read the long Genesis passage for this session. Jot down the various strained relationships you see in Laban's extended family. Where have you seen similar family struggles?
2. Read Mark 7:9-13. What does the word *corban* mean?
3. Think of personality traits or habits that you or others bring into your family that cause upheaval and brokenness among family members. How can the conflict be resolved? Bring your insights to the covenant meeting.
4. If possible, read an advice column in your newspaper three days in a row. Note the number of family conflicts you see. What advice would you give?

Understanding

Among all the shapes and sizes of families, it is virtually impossible to find a family that has not encountered severe stress, alienation between children and adults, loss of life and property, separation or divorce, elderly parent problems, abuse, serious illness, or family jealousies.

In his prayer book called *Children's Letters to God,* David Heller recorded this prayer from Derek, age eleven: "Dear God, a lot of folks say there is too much rough stuff on TV and too much killing too. I say there is too much rough and tough stuff and killing in the Bible. Make my day." Derek is right. The Bible tells of a lot of pain and brokenness in family relationships. The Jacob and Laban story in Genesis 29:1—30:30 is a prime example of an alienated, broken family. But the good news of both the Old and the New Testaments is that God uses even, or especially, the broken families to give grace.

We often have a naive view of the Bible, a child's view of the people in Sunday school stories. God's family and chosen people are heroic to us and sacred. But family blood lines don't necessarily guarantee freedom from pain and brokenness, even if it's God's family. This Jacob and Laban story is a case of deep brokenness in the family God chose.

Dishonesty

Laban is Jacob's uncle who promises to give Jacob his daughter Rachel in exchange for seven years of labor. His word to Jacob, however, was not as good as his bond. The seven years of laboring for Rachel seemed to Jacob "but a few days because of the love he had for her" (29:20), but when pay day came, Laban tricked Jacob. It wasn't wife-swapping that Laban engaged in, but daughter-switching. On the night Jacob and Rachel were to be joined, Laban gave his daughter Leah instead, under cloak of darkness. In the morning Jacob discovered his bride was not Rachel. "What is this you have done to me?" he asked (29:25). Laban explained that the older daughter must be married first. Since Jacob likely would not have agreed to the substitute wife, Laban switched the two sisters to follow custom.

Families do not operate well when someone is dishonest. Even children sense the importance of honesty as a family value. When the father of a four-year-old continually broke his promise to come to his former wife's home and take the child on outings, she pointed out frankly to her mother at the breakfast table one morning, "Daddy lies. He says he loves me and will pick me up, but he doesn't come." Dishonesty breaks down family trust. Jacob agreed to work another seven years for Rachel but he had lost confidence in Laban.

Jealousy

Jealousy also weakened Jacob's family structure. Jacob eventually married both sisters, which solved Laban's problem of marrying off his daughters in the proper order. But it raised many other problems as the sisters continually vied for Jacob's affection. In turn, the competition led to envy and baiting. When Leah discovered that Rachel could not conceive, she had even more children with Jacob to make her sister jealous. Each son's name, such as Fortune and Happy, was Leah's attempt to lord her successes over her sister.

When Rachel saw that she was being outdone in bearing children, she became angry and said to Jacob, "Give me children, or I shall die!" (30:1). Like Sarah, Rachel is barren and must give her maid, Bilhah, to her husband, Jacob, to produce heirs. Through Bilhah, Jacob and Rachel had several sons. The names Rachel gave to them, such as God Judged and Wrestling, also reveal the jealousies between sisters.

After several rounds of vindictive childbearing, Rachel's womb was opened and Joseph was born. It would be through Joseph that the family would be reconciled many years later, but not before great damage was done to many family members.

While it seems cruel for Leah to taunt Rachel, we should remember that social custom played a big part in this broken family just as it did in Abraham and Sarah's family. Some of the friction was beyond the control of the characters in the story. For one, an Old Testament woman's worth was determined by her ability to produce children, as we see in the Leah and Rachel stories. Infertility was a disgrace. Moreover, boy babies were considered superior to girl babies since males contained the "seed" of the family line. And do not forget that the entire problem in Jacob's family began because of the convention of marrying off the oldest daughter before younger daughters could be married. All of these customs worked against Leah as well as Rachel and were more responsible for the alienation than the two sisters.

Perhaps there are cultural expectations that cause jealousy and envy in the modern world as well. Many families still give honor to oldest sons and hope that their oldest child will marry first. We have expectations that our children will marry within a certain class structure, a certain race, or a certain religious family. We hope that they will fulfill our dreams by becoming successful, wealthy, and happy. We are stumped when a millionaire like Millard Fuller defies expectations, gives away all his money, and starts up Habitat for Humanity to build houses for the poor. Such violation of custom doesn't happen very often.

Customs around inheritance and family gifts also cause many family jealousies. Birthrights, inheritance, and offerings created disappointments and envy in several Bible families. It does the same in modern families. One family promised each son a new car on his sixteenth birthday. When the younger son turned sixteen, he anxiously awaited his birthday and the set of car keys he knew he would receive at dinner. When the time came, he opened the gift and found a Bible in the box instead of keys. Disappointed and enraged, the boy flung the Bible to the floor and stormed out of the room. The father, angered by the boy's disrespect and greed, refused to speak to his son. The father and son did not speak ever again. When the father died, the son came home to help sort through his father's possessions. Among his father's things, the son found the Bible that was given to him on his sixteenth birthday. When he leafed through the pages, he found a check in the amount of a car, dated on his sixteenth birthday. Jealousy, stubbornness, and greed are terrible wedges that drive family members apart.

Cultural Tradition

A third cause for disruption in the family of Laban was the insistence upon following a cultural tradition regardless of its consequences. When Jacob discovered on his wedding night that the graceful and beautiful girl he really loved (29:17) was replaced in the bridal suite by her older sister, he said to his father-in-law, "What is this you have done to me? Did I not serve with you for Rachel? Why then have you deceived me?" (29:25).

Laban said, "This is not done in our country—giving the younger before the firstborn" (29:26). Jacob seemed satisfied with Laban's answer and agreed to work another seven years for Rachel. Traditions can be beautiful and can provide rituals and memories that bring solidarity, warmth, and closeness in families. However, traditions that over time become separated from their purpose give rise to alienation.

A young woman who grew up in a Protestant family dated a young Roman Catholic man. They talked about marriage, but the fiancee's mother threatened that if her daughter did not marry a

Protestant in the tradition of her family, she would not plan the wedding or attend. The couple decided to marry despite the mother's objections, believing they did not have to have the mother's blessing in order to make a marriage and a family. But the mother's dismay drove a wedge in their relationship, splitting the daughter's loyalty between parent and spouse. Numerous counseling sessions ended in gridlock. After a period of six painful years, both the daughter's and parents' marriages ended in divorce.

Laban and Jacob called a truce in their wrangling only after years had gone by and every trick had been tried, including sheep stealing. But God chose this messed up family to accomplish divine plans. Through Joseph, God sent the message of grace to Egypt and back. To this contentious bunch, Joseph was able to bring reconciliation and peace.

Wrangling over Parents

The Leah and Rachel conflict was between adults who argued about children. But families are also split over the opposite problem—what to do about aging parents. Who will decide when parents should no longer drive? Who should decide that parents need to move to a retirement home? Who should decide who gets a parent's possessions. Who decides which child shall pay for daycare for the elderly and who shall pay for medicines? How will the parents, children, and grandchildren feel that everything is fair? Mark 7:9-13 deals with this issue that often creates tensions in families.

In this text, Jesus is critical of religious people who meticulously keep up the traditions of the faith, but neglect their moral responsibilities. Jesus was famous for debating with the elders and leaders about which was more important, the letter of the law or the spirit of the law. In the case of elderly parents, the traditionalists might argue that a person's first priority is to keep the commandments, even if it means ignoring other aspects of life. Jesus says, however, that everything we do, not just the things we do at the temple, should reflect our faith.

Corban was a temple offering, a gift for God. People of Jesus' time were evidently shunning financial obligations to family, claiming they had given all they had at the temple. After corban, there was nothing left for elderly parents. But one of God's commandments is "Honor your father and your mother, so that your days may be long in the land that the Lord your God is giving you" (Exod.

20:12). Jesus said, "You have a fine way of rejecting the commandment of God in order to keep your tradition!" (Mark 7:9).

A major source of brokenness in families is the scandalous way we treat our elderly relatives. Children may not give all their money to corban, but they give most of their time and energy to their own pursuits, leaving very little quality time for the oldest members of the family.

In Katie Fund Wiebe's book, *Prayers of an Omega*, an elderly man talks to God about his recent decision to give up driving, much to the relief of his children. But he laments that he will soon be at the mercy of children who have little time for him.

> The children say they'll take me anywhere I need to go. Just phone and they'll come. But my longing to see that lilac tree welcome the spring disappears when I have to squeeze a passing look at it between a dentist's appointment and a quick trip to the post office to catch the last mail. Middle-aged children haven't got time for nature's all-out shout of welcome in spring just yet.

Even under the best of circumstances and the most loving of homes, care of the elderly can put strains on families. Children live at great distances from their parents these days. Looking after parents in another state or province or even in another town means frequent trips or hiring staff to do the jobs children would normally do for parents. If parents suffer from medical conditions or have a change in personality or loss of memory, daily care can become burdensome and a resentment.

In the worst circumstances, siblings are alienated from elderly parents or from each other over parental issues. Everyone knows a family that is split over ancient animosities or unfair divisions of a parent's wealth. One child feels as if all the eldercare is left up to her because the parents slighted her brother once upon a time and he refuses to help. Or brothers and sisters stop speaking after the reading of the will because one child received more than the others. Family brokenness may last long after parents are gone.

Reconciliation may also come long after a parent is gone. Imagine a situation like this. John worked all his life to have a relationship with his irresponsible, mentally ill father. When his friends said, "Forget about your dad," he refused. His father would always be his father and he longed to be a family. Then one night, John's father was hit by a car and killed. All possibility of connecting with his dad was gone.

In the days that followed the death, John's relatives charged the driver with involuntary manslaughter and sued for hundreds of thousands of dollars. He knew, however, that his father was suicidal and had probably stepped in front of the car to end his miserable life. Meanwhile, the man who hit him was hospitalized with a heart attack brought on by anxiety, extreme guilt, and remorse. Feeling that his dad would not have wanted the driver to suffer, John went to the police with the true story and talked with the driver to relieve his guilt.

While the family blamed John for depriving them of a monetary settlement, he felt reconciled to his dad. He connected with his father in death as he never had in life.

Healing Brokenness

How can we bind up broken families? The church is a perfect place for healing of all kinds, including healing family brokenness. God can use the patient, loving hands of the congregation to minister to broken families, helping them to heal or at least cope with tough situations. The first thing the congregation must do is listen for the cries of the hurting and caringly initiate conversation with broken families. As the Bible suggests, "Bear one another's burdens, and in this way you will fulfill the law of Christ" (Gal. 6:2-5).

Listening and loving are important tools for working with broken families, but some action is also necessary. Courses such as this one help people understand the dynamics of family and improve communication. When a family communicates well, it can work through many of its tough situations. If necessary, pastors, counselors, and mentors in the congregation can intervene in family situations to clarify issues, identify problems, and guide families to better communication. As a third party, an outsider can often help move the healing process along without getting caught in jealousies, animosities, or misunderstandings.

The church is also the place where people are challenged to change and where they are forgiven when their efforts fall short. Family bonds in both well and ailing families motivate us to try over and over to make it work even when it might not. We may never be able to solve age-old problems, such as the need for approval from parents who cannot give it, or the temptation to give advice to children to save them from grief, even if they don't want it. Still families keep on trying to make family work. Like the quest for faith, the effort to make a family work is an unending process that takes a lot of effort, endures a lot of heartbreak, needs a lot of grace, and provides a whole lot of joy.

Discussion and Action

1. If you are able, tell about some pain and brokenness you have experienced in your family. What grace have you experienced in the midst of family pain?
2. What personality traits do you or others bring to your family that spark conflict? How does your family handle these incidences? Does identifying the sources of conflict help you deal with bitter situations better? How? Give examples.
3. The Jacob and Laban story reveals several strains in the historic family—jealousy over one man, competition, in-law problems, the custom of marrying off the oldest daughter first, and the preference for boy babies. Give examples of these same problems in modern families.
4. Painful and alienating experiences in families are not exhausted in this writing. Name others. Then talk about ways God is walking with people in these situations. Where do you see grace for families?
5. Consider suggesting to a worship committee or pastor that the church invite people to write speeches on the theme "Struggle and Pain in Families: How the Church Can Help." For a sermon on a family Sunday, allow the pastor to use two complete speeches or excerpts from each speech.

5

Brothers, Sisters, Siblings
Genesis 37:1-36; Luke 10:38-42

Each child in a family is blessed with a unique personality, physical appearance, and ability. While this variety makes life interesting, it is also the source of friction and rivalry. The stories of Joseph and his brothers and Mary and Martha show that sibling rivalry is common, even in the Bible. They also show us how to accommodate difference and still love each other.

Personal Preparation

1. Read the story of Joseph, his brothers, and their father in Genesis 37:1-36. Then read chapters 42—45 to see how the brothers are reconciled. Summarize what you read. With which brother do you identify?
2. What difference does it make that you are the oldest, youngest, middle, or the only child in your family?
3. Reminisce about your siblings. Think about the fun, love and competitiveness between you.
4. For more Bible stories about sibling rivalry, read the Cain and Abel story (Gen. 4:1-16), the story of Tamar and her brothers (2 Sam. 13), and Jacob and Esau (Gen. 25:19-34).

Understanding

Darling newborn babies grow up. The innocent, helpless infant who burrows into the crook of your neck and shoulder, almost becoming one with you, grows and develops a personality of its own. Very early in life, its character sets a course and the child begins to assert the traits it will have all of its life. The helpless infant, who *seems* so much like every infant, is very different from others. Even brothers and sisters, who share some common genetic makeup, can be markedly different depending on circumstance and biology. It is not long at all before the needs, abilities, and personality of a child begin butting up against the needs, abilities, and personalities of other children, especially against brothers and sisters in the same family.

Sibling Rivalry

If their children clash, if children feel treated unequally or resent the amount of attention a brother or sister receives, some parents may feel as if they have failed at parenting. It is difficult, however, for parents to treat each child equally, for too many differences and circumstances exist. In fact, treating children equally could feel like an injustice to one or more children in a family. If, for instance, one child in a family has a learning disability and only receives as much help with homework as the other children receive, he or she is probably not receiving enough help. Should children expect equal treatment from parents? Is it possible for brothers and sisters to be compatible?

Although the Bible doesn't tell us much about most contemporary issues, it does have a lot to say about sibling rivalry. From the story of Cain and Abel to Jesus' parable of the two sons, the Bible tells of struggles between brothers and sisters. This lesson looks at the stories of two families: Joseph's brothers who are jealous about their father's special treatment of him, the youngest brother; and the sisters, Mary and Martha, who have to make their opposite personalities work together. These stories demonstrate that brothers and sisters cannot expect equality, but if they are willing to accept differences, they will be able to love their brother or sister as the Lord loves the variety of people in the family of God. A family of four grown children began talking at a holiday gathering about their childhood. Somewhere in the conversation, the recollection of fond memories turned to frank discussion about which child was the favorite. The three older children revealed that for a long time they perceived the youngest, the "baby" of the family, to be the favorite, the one who could do no wrong. The oldest, like many first children, believed he had too many constraints; the second tested every boundary and felt she had disappointed her parents; the third got lost between the exasperating second child and the darling baby; but the baby was cute, obedient, and eager to please. Joseph had somewhat the same problem. He was the youngest of eleven children and the first son of his father's favorite wife. Not surprisingly, his place of honor in the family made his ten brothers jealous.

Joseph and His Brothers

The whole Bible story, the entire history of the Hebrews, depended on Abraham's descendants prevailing. Those who looked back to Jacob as their forefather were destined to greatness not through any chances of human history, but because God ordained it that way. This train of thought runs through the story of Jacob and his sons. Whatever happened to Jacob or through Jacob was predestined to be. Thus, as horrible as the brothers' treatment of Joseph was, the story must provide a way for Joseph to get to Egypt to save the remnant of Hebrews for the future.

It is clear that the brothers were not motivated by the will of God. They wanted to send Joseph to Egypt because they felt slighted. The youngest brother, Joseph, was the heir to the family wealth and their father's favorite son. In Middle Eastern culture, birthrights and blessings were special for the oldest son in a family, and Jacob's eldest son felt as if he was the one who would inherit the family fortune. Birthrights meant leadership of the family and a double share of the inheritance. Deuteronomy 21:15-17 lays down the law on this. "If a man has two wives, one of them loved and the other disliked, and if both the loved and the disliked have borne him sons, the firstborn being the son of the one who is disliked, then on the day when he wills his possessions to his sons, he is not permitted to treat the son of the loved as the firstborn in preference to the son of the disliked, who is firstborn."

Blessings were also part of an oldest son's inheritance in Israelite culture. Deathbed blessings were important in the life and literature of ancient peoples (see Gen. 49; Josh. 23). It was believed that the blessing, like the curse, released a power that effectively determined the character and destiny of the recipient which could not be retracted. It may have seemed to the brothers that Joseph also undeservedly received the blessings that were meant for the oldest brother.

While Hebrew law dictated rights for the eldest son, many Bible families, beginning with Adam and Eve, gave preference to their younger sons. Abel's gift was more worthy than Cain's; Jacob, instead of his older brother Esau, obtained the family birthright; and David was chosen from among eleven older brothers to be king of Israel. In God's story, the tables are often turned so that the last is first and the first last. God rarely gives us what we deserve according to age, virtue, or position. God gives us what we need. Therefore, age has no special privilege. God calls on those who are weak and powerless. Joseph's brothers were jealous of the favor and blessing he received from his father, believing that they should have been rewarded for their age as the law prescribed.

When Jacob gave Joseph a long royal robe as a special gift for his favorite son, the coat set off a tide of sibling resentment toward Joseph that had been growing for some time. "They hated him, and could not speak peaceably to him" (37:4b).

As in Joseph's family, it's a reality that families have favorite children. Through no fault of the parents, some children are easier to get along with or are better at relating, and they are the ones who seem to be, or are, favorites. No one advocates love for one child to the exclusion of the others, but the truth is that we all feel degrees of love or different kinds of love for different members of the family.

It's too bad that Joseph believed the love elevated him above the others in importance. As Joseph told his brothers about his dreams, he flaunted his favor in front of them, expecting them to treat him like a king. His father, who had declared his favor for Joseph, is as disgusted with Joseph's arrogance as are the brothers. So Jacob demands Joseph to stop irritating the others with his delusions of grandeur.

Unfortunately, the brothers suffer for years, believing that life has truly been unfair to them. Joseph will be more successful according to God's plan, and they must come to terms with reality. The jealous brothers who sold Joseph into slavery eventually discover that they need him to survive. They find they must work out a relationship with him and settle their own relationship with their father. The story ends well. Joseph matures in his years in Egypt where he is humbled by his life as a slave and prisoner. When his brothers finally come to him for help, he resists being overcome with revenge and genuinely wants to help them. His brothers (who at least felt some guilt and spared their brother from death) finally learn to accept Joseph for who he is. They also learned from their mistakes, as Jacob does *not*. Jacob repeats his mistake, choosing a new favorite, his twelfth son, Benjamin. But the brothers do not become angry again as they had with Joseph.

How we cope with inequalities in families is difficult. Resentments easily rise to the top when parents require much from older children but relax standards for younger children. Jealousies bubble up when needy children get a lot of attention. Troubles arise when difficult personalities compete with charming personalities for parental love. Coping is a matter of coming to terms with the differences in families and avoiding the comparisons that make siblings feel inadequate. Parents will cope better if they feel less guilt for treating children differently and try hard to communicate love to each child in the most appropriate way for that child. They will do better to give children equivalent love rather than equal love.

Mary and Martha

Mary and Martha are also sibling rivals, but they are not struggling for their parents' favor. They are opposites in personality trying to get along. In her book, *Just a Sister Away,* Renita Weems speculates about what Martha is thinking after her outburst against her sister, Mary. Martha says,

> I suppose the only way I know how to express my love and concern is by cleaning and fussing, for I've never known the luxury of self-contemplation. Mary, by contrast, is quiet, sensitive, and at times given to unusual outbursts of affection. Take, for example, the time she stunned everyone by anointing Jesus' feet with expensive oil and then wiping his feet with her hair. Only a slave does such a thing! I was aghast! Yet, admittedly, her sensitivity and her humility touched even my heart.

Martha was the one who wanted order, the kind who would search endlessly for the one-cent error in the check book. Mary, on the other hand, liked to wonder at the sayings of Jesus that had no clear cut answers. The two types irritated each other from time to time, but they also combined to provide for Jesus' every need, his physical comfort and his spiritual life.

Most people probably identify with Martha. The Marthas of the world are dutiful, hard working, and prefer doing things the way they "ought" to be done. But nearly every family has a Mary, a brother or sister who cares nothing for order and convention. The mixture of the two personalities is like oil and water. Brothers and sisters who are like Mary and Martha will fight over simple things, such as irritating mannerisms, how to keep order, how to divide chores, or anything that doesn't suit one or the other. The small irritations keep them from seeing any value in having differences or determining how they might complement each other.

Renita Weems continues the fictional monologue of Martha:

> In the end both of us were wrong: Mary, for taking me for granted; and I, for not going to her personally to voice my complaint. My Lord, how easy it is for sisters to abuse one another!

Cain and Abel

In some families, the differences may indicate serious, lifelong problems. There are many brothers and sisters who struggle with how to relate to delinquent siblings, siblings with addictions, and siblings with behavior problems. Very often, families don't know how to make a relationship out of these monumental differences and find it easier to sever a relationship or deny the problem than to work at it.

The brothers Cain and Abel were also different. Cain tilled and Abel herded sheep. Together they could provide everything to sustain the family, but jealousy actually drove Cain to kill his brother, destroying the whole. When families have differences as great as Cain and Abel's, they should get help to bring the relationships back into shape.

Growing Pains

No doubt parents would like to find solutions to sibling rivalry and its countless arguments and hurt feelings. No one can eliminate the frictions between siblings, unfortunately, but friction can be reduced if siblings try not to take each other for granted and are frank with each other when something goes wrong. Simple rules of communication, including honest appreciation of differences, can help families use their tensions for good and encourage uniqueness instead of stifling it.

Two brothers, John and Mark, fought with each other physically until fingers were broken and noses were bloody. John was older, a quiet kid who knew how to get someone's goat and watch the frustration rise. He kept all his emotion inside and seemingly knew how to control every feeling, every relationship, and every situation. Mark, who was younger, was continually trying to best his brother to earn John's respect. But Mark was a scrapper who had very little self-control. Quick to anger and easily provoked, Mark would land on his brother in a rage, punching, kicking, and biting. Their father demanded apologies, but neither boy detected any sincerity in the other's words. Their fighting episodes continued well into their teen years, then changed to verbal exchanges as they grew to adulthood.

John became a policeman, which provided a professional outlet for his style of control. He married but resisted becoming a parent, because raising children was too unpredictable. He became a father anyway and has learned to love it and to let go of his control in small ways, something like his brother. Mark works for social service agencies in which he daily deals with people's pain and brokenness. He has learned to control some of his feeling, something like his brother, so that he can work with tough social problems without taking them all on himself.

The two brothers did not sit down one afternoon to work out their problems or agree to appreciate each other. It happened because they could not undo the bond that forms simply because they are brothers. Gradually they learned how to live together harmoniously and to see that together they made up a whole family that both loved freely and guarded love before it became meaningless.

Bible scholar Fred Craddock says that "if we were to ask Jesus which example applies to us, the Samaritan [Martha] or Mary, his answer would probably be Yes."

Discussion and Action

1. Bring up the sibling rivalries of your growing years. Are you still affected by them? How?
2. How can parents recognize children's different gifts without causing jealousy or favoritism?
3. How can adult children forgive parents and siblings for hurt feelings left over from childhood?
4. Invite a local child psychologist to help you teach children to be friends and to solve conflict.
5. Compare the experiences of people in the group who are first children, youngest children, middle children, or only children.
6. What is healthy about your relationship with adult siblings now? Talk about what is still unresolved if you can.
7. In what ways have you succeeded in helping your own children have a healthy relationship? Plan a time to discuss with your children their feelings or memories of their sibling relationships. If a confessional or celebrative time is needed, have it!

6

Respecting Boundaries
2 Samuel 11:1—12:1a
Matthew 5:27-30

The poet Robert Frost said in the poem "Mending Wall" that "good fences make good neighbors." Letting people know clearly what our sexual and social boundaries are and honoring the boundaries of others makes good sense. But more than good sense, respecting boundaries is a biblical teaching found in the story of King David and in the Sermon on the Mount among other places.

Personal Preparation

1. Read 2 Samuel 11:1—12:1a. Think about your boundaries, your own limits of decency. Also, pay attention to the way you treat other people's boundaries. Read Psalm 51, David's psalm of repentance.
2. For possible grist for group discussion, list limits that are easy for you to respect. List those that are in the hazy or more difficult areas.
3. Reread the story of David and Bathsheba several times. Read it once picturing Bathsheba as a willing partner in the affair. Read it again picturing Bathsheba as an unwilling partner. Also think of David once as a forceful man, demanding that Bathsheba come to him. Then, as you read the story again, think of David as a sensitive man who feels remorse. Which combination seems most likely to you?

4. Read Jesus' teaching in Matthew 5:27-30. What guidance does this passage give you?

Understanding

The sexual behavior of everyone from evangelists to a U.S. Supreme Court justice has been under intense public scrutiny lately. But sexual ethics, marital fidelity, and the use and abuse of power in and out of family relationships is a problem that is as old as the scriptures themselves. When God comes to the people of Israel living in Egypt, they are victims of power. It was God's intent to free people from abuses at the hands of others so that they could live fully as the people of God. The theme of power appears frequently in the Bible—when people have too much of it, God confounds them. When they have too little of it, God comes to their aid. God, however, ultimately holds the power. The Ten Commandments, given by God to the Israelites through their leader Moses, help us remember that it was God who rescued us and that our power has limits.

Families operate with many limits, but in this session, we will look only at sexual boundaries, both inside and outside marriage relationships. The story of David and Bathsheba is a case in which David carries out his desires and crosses real boundaries outside his marriage vows. The passage from Matthew is a teaching on lust, which, Jesus argues, also violates boundaries, because once a person becomes consumed with desire for someone other than a spouse, that person has already abandoned the marital relationship in spirit.

David and Bathsheba

In 2 Samuel 11, we witness a dramatic episode in the life of King David, who is one of God's greatest servants one minute and a miserable sinner the next. One day, David arose from a late afternoon nap and went for a walk on the palace roof. His eyes came to rest on a beautiful woman taking a bath nearby. Later he found out she was the wife of Uriah who was away at the time, fighting in David's army during one of the spring tribal battles. One look was not enough. David allowed himself to become a voyeur, fixing his stare on Bathsheba. From a distance he began to desire Bathsheba and lust after her. Even though an informant told him that Bathsheba was married, David disregarded the sacredness of the neighbor's marriage. Despite his own marital commitments (at the time he had six of his seven wives with him in the royal palace), he acted on impulse, ordering Bathsheba to come to the palace where he had a relationship with her. Some time later, Bathsheba discovered she was pregnant, complicating the couple's sin.

As a cover-up David disregarded basic human decency by trying to place his guilt upon Uriah. One sin led to another. When a complimentary army leave and a staged drunken party didn't bring results, David broke another moral barrier. He plotted Uriah's death on the battlefield to resemble a natural result of infighting. Again King David used his power of status to invade the privacy of another to satisfy his own ego and to cover up weaknesses he refused to admit.

David clearly crossed the boundary of trust and propriety and then used deceit to cover his sin. But what about Bathsheba? The text does not tell us if she came to David willingly and if she intentionally broke her marriage vow to Uriah. Sometimes Bathsheba is seen as a seductress, knowingly bathing in view of the king to arouse him. But all we know for sure is that David took another man's wife. If she wanted to refuse, she could not, because David had more power than she, which he seemed perfectly willing to use.

As king, David is the one appointed to look after the people, but in the case of Bathsheba and Uriah, David betrays a fundamental trust. It happens today too. People with power or authority or responsibility to help and protect people use their position to take advantage of others. Therapists, doctors, clergy, teachers, and others betray the trust of people in their charge. They cross the boundary to take what they want and they have the ability to make the other person comply.

In his book *Sex in the Forbidden Zone,* psychiatrist Peter Rutter interviewed men and women about the things that drive people to betray the trust placed in them.

> Most of [the] women, in trying to account for the reasons they participated in sex with a therapist, pastor, or mentor, despite feeling how wrong it was, also cited the strong influence of cultural factors in their upbringing that steered them toward complying with the sexual desires of these powerful men. They felt that the force of this preexisting message encouraging compliance, when combined with their inner need to hold onto the

extraordinary promise offered in the relationship, set up a psychological trap they were powerless to resist.

Women like Bathsheba are not powerless to guard their boundaries, but they are under enormous pressure at times to give in to men who want to violate their boundaries. By holding jobs, grades, secrets, and authority over women, men can easily cross boundaries.

When David is confronted by the prophet Nathan for his deeds, he discovers the consequences of betrayal, deceit, and sin. It is not just Bathsheba and Uriah he has violated. David has violated God's good purpose by using his power to overpower Bathsheba and kill Uriah. David has put his own carnal desires ahead of God and his mission to shepherd the people.

As with any other pleasure, sex can be addictive. It can make people lose sight of all other important parts of life. Sometimes husbands and wives place a value on their sexual intimacy that eclipses concern for their children, their faith, and their personal well-being. It is estimated that twenty percent of Americans and thirty percent of clergy are sexually addicted. If the romance of marriage is insufficient, the sexually addicted person will look elsewhere without qualms.

Perhaps David is sexually addicted. He desires this relationship with Bathsheba over everything else, even God. As a result, he faces a future of trouble and grief. Nathan tells David that, considering his offenses, he deserves to die, but because he has repented he is forgiven.

Psalm 51 is considered to be David's confession for his failures to respect the limits of right living and forgetting God. It is a moving account of a person's deep repentance. It is a heart-longing appeal for healing and a new heart. Knowing all this, we wonder, how could a man after God's own heart get so far off limits?

So how did King David get into this mess? At first, he simply gazed at Bathsheba and was tempted. This is common to all people and not necessarily a sin. Next was the lustful thought, committing the act in his mind. Lust is the lobby or vestibule for sin and should be barred because it lets the thought of action enter in and take hold. Then there is the decision to act. That is the sin.

Jesus' Interpretation

This leads us into Jesus' teaching in Matthew 5:27-30: "You have heard that it was said" (5:27). Where have we heard this? In the Ten

Commandments. Jesus recites God's law for the Hebrews, including the seventh commandment: "You shall not commit adultery." Jesus reminds the people as they listen to him on the mountainside that God forbade the act of crossing forbidden sexual boundaries. Clearly, the Levitical holiness code attaches punishment for violation of the commandments. "If a man is caught lying with the wife of another man, both of them shall die" (Deut. 22:22).

Then Jesus goes on to give his interpretation of the old law: "But I say to you that everyone who looks at a woman with lust has already committed adultery with her in his heart." The obsession with someone who is not your wife or husband causes you to forsake a devotion to your spouse. Already you have broken your relationship in spirit. Brokenness begins, not with sexual intimacy, but with the lustful thought, a longing look, and the touch of the hand. Not only the forbidden action defies boundaries but also the forbidden thought is guilty in the sight of God.

How shall we handle these temptations? By a kind of inner surgery that extracts the offensive thoughts. "If your right eye causes you to sin, tear it out and throw it away; it is better for you" (5:29). Jesus advocates stringent discipline as we seek to live in the realm of right relationships. Important questions to ask ourselves as people of the covenant are: As we emphasize in our relationships with others the need to love, support, affirm, praise, and understand them, are we diminishing the need to exercise in those relationships stringent, exacting, firm, and careful discipline? Do we claim that temptation overpowers us as if our faith and devotion to God is not stronger?

Be certain of this, that Jesus' demand for carefulness in the way we approach boundaries with others is not for repression but for fulfillment. Dr. Peter Rutter helpfully points out that discipline is not a form of deprivation. He tells us, rather, that we gain by self-discipline.

> If we have been working together for some time, a familiarity and trust develops between us that starts to erode the boundaries of seemingly impersonal professional relationships.... Under these conditions, images of sexual union flood us.... Yet every time I have found myself caught up in sexual fantasies about a patient, I have discovered that something holds me back—not just a rule against sexual contact, but a feeling that

something of value will be destroyed if that line is crossed.

That "something of value" is a relationship to a spouse, trust of clients, respect for people who come for healing, personal integrity, respect for the most humane values of one's profession, personal discipline, and commitment to upholding God's purposes instead of one's own.

The accounts of marriage commitments that fail altogether when one of the partners falls in love with someone else are innumerable. Everyone knows a story like the typical tale of the man and woman who marry after college with great plans for the future. But life settles into an unglamorous routine. Children come along. Women become frustrated with childcare. The man works each day and has many contacts outside the home. His business contacts are more challenging and stimulating than his relationship with his wife. When he works closely with a female associate at the office, he begins to imagine a life with her. What would it be like to be with this exciting person all the time? Soon, the imaginable becomes possible and then true.

Something of Value

No part of family life is successful without clear communication. Couples who cannot voice their frustrations and disappointments may grow away from a relationship and lose respect for boundaries when they lose contact with their partner. Without communication, one partner will often drift into someone else's sphere, someone who provides what a spouse lacks. It is important to work on communication early in a marriage and to keep talking to avoid a broken relationship.

Discipline over desires will also help marriage partners honor the boundaries to which they have committed themselves. A young man who was separated from his wife was an easy target for a single young woman in his neighborhood, rebounding from a divorce. She wanted to have a sexual relationship with him, but he had the sense to say, "I have made many mistakes in my marriage. If I hope to reclaim it, I do not want to have to try to overcome infidelity in addition to all the other hurts."

When husbands and wives have crossed boundaries, it is difficult to reestablish trust. It is difficult to find trust again even when one partner has grown apart from the other and entertains affairs only

Respecting Boundaries

in his or her head. But it can be done. The most powerful motivating factor for respecting the boundaries of Christian marriage is that God's purpose is to guard, cherish, and protect us as a people in a covenant of faith. We also ought to guard, cherish, and protect each other in covenant with one another.

Discussion and Action

1. Which teachings of the Bible have helped you understand the limits and boundaries of marriage? "You shall not covet. . . . You shall not commit adultery. . . . You shall not kill" or Jesus' words, "You have heard that it was said . . . but I say to you . . . "? Ponder why a commandment like the following was not included in the decalogue: "You shall not abuse one another"?
2. When have you felt like Dr. Rutter when he said, "I have discovered that something holds me back"?
3. Does the level of trust and confidentiality in your group provide enough security for you to share your list of limits which you prepared before coming? If so, share them.
4. Nathan only became involved in David's case after the deed was done. Should a third party intervene? At what point should someone intervene in a struggling relationship?
5. What for you will be destroyed if you cross a sexual boundary? What happens to you when someone crosses your boundary?
6. What other types of boundaries are there in families? Does the Bible tell us about other boundaries?
7. How can someone who violates a boundary be helped? How can the victim whose boundary has been violated be helped?
8. How can marriages be repaired after boundaries are violated and trust broken?

7

When Parents Fail
Judges 11:29-40; Mark 10:13-16

Childlikeness may bring on the kingdom of heaven, but in many families, being a child means enduring psychological and physical abuse. Abusive parents use violence to consolidate their power over children, and Christian parents sometimes do it under the guise of faithfulness.

Personal Preparation

1. Read Judges 11:29-40, imagining that you are Jephthah. Reread it and imagine that you are Jephthah's daughter. How does the story strike you each time?
2. Think about the kind of relationship you, as a child, had with your parents. How has it changed?
3. When does discipline cross the line to become abuse in your mind? How were you disciplined as a child?
4. Read Mark 10:13-16. What does it mean to you to receive the kingdom as a little child?

Understanding

Abuse is any mistreatment or neglect of a child that results in harm or injury. It can include physical abuse (purposely injuring a child by hitting, kicking, shaking); emotional abuse (crushing a child's spirit with verbal attacks, threats, humiliation); sexual abuse (sexual contact, inappropriate touching, obscene pictures and language); or neglect (willfully failing to provide for a child's emotional and physical needs, failing to offer guidance). Nearly two million children suffer from child abuse each year. These incidents occur in households across the entire economic, religious and social spectrum. Because child abuse hurts children and everyone else too, it is imperative that congregations and families use the many available resources for understanding, preventing and healing abusive behavior.

An energetic nine-year-old boy with a beaming face said in a youth club discussion, "I hope our home will always be a happy place where I can have fun and where Daddy and Mommy will show me how to do things right." That's a hopeful comment for a youth soon to enter the twenty-first century. Not all children would agree. Their homes are full of sadness, sickness, and abuse. The family is where life is shaped, where children learn to relate to others, where there is a chance to develop faith, where character takes shape. What we become in later years is largely determined by our home environment. Why, when the technological world around us makes huge advances, do we lumber along in human relations, making the same mistakes over and over, especially in parent-child relationships? And why do Christian families fail at healthy relationships between parents and children at the same rate as everyone else?

Christians are susceptible to the same weaknesses as everyone, but we have a resource—our faith—that can help us restore wholeness and health to family relationships. The story of Jephthah's daughter helps us see the way that we easily fall into abusive behavior, all in the name of God. Learning the pitfalls of Christian parenting from Jephthah can help us avoid the same mistakes and look upon children as models of true faithful living.

Jephthah's Daughter

The Book of Judges in the Old Testament is a compilation of transitional stories of the Israelites. The age of the great leaders Moses and Joshua was gone. The rule of King David was yet to come. During this period of changeover, numerous charismatic leaders appeared, as they do in any era of great change, jockeying for position. The various Israelite tribes were engaged in military skirmishes with other tribes over land the Israelites confiscated in the great conquest of Canaan.

Among these leaders was Jephthah, who came to be a successful warrior despite a miserable youth. Jephthah was the son of Gilead and a prostitute. Though Jephthah lived with his father and was raised with Gilead's "legitimate" sons, he was eventually rejected. His half brothers forced him out of their home and barred him from his share of the family inheritance. The embittered boy fled to a town called Tob.

Alone in the world, Jephthah loved himself when no one else would. With a survivalist mentality, he sought security in power and adoration in notoriety. He formed an army of marauding mercenaries and made a name for himself as a skilled commander.

When the tribe of Gilead got into a tribal disagreement with the Ammonites, the tribal elders felt they needed a tough-minded leader to get them out of their jam. Having heard that their brother Jephthah had become mighty and unbeatable, they invited him to command the Gileadite army. His response was one of sarcasm. "Are you not the very ones who rejected me and drove me out of my father's house? So why do you come to me now when you are in trouble?" (11:7). But Jephthah saw the opportunity to prove his superiority to his brothers and took on the job.

In what seems like an act of pious devotion to God, Jephthah promises to make a burnt offering of the first person he sees when he returns home, if God will only let him win the battle with the Ammonites. His promise, however, is not to glorify God, but to glorify himself. Jephthah hopes to show his brothers how wrong they were to reject him. He wants them to know how much they need him. He wants to show that he is a great general.

His vow resulted in a victory on the battlefield and a tragedy at home. Jephthah believed he could not retract a vow to God even when it was his beloved daughter, his only child, who came through the doors dancing, overjoyed to see her father. Perhaps Jephthah assumed that one of the servants would come through first. Even so, he promised to sacrifice another human being for his own gain. That he would consider sacrificing his own child underscores his bent for power no matter how he got it.

The Cycle of Abuse

Chances are that child abusers today were abused in their own childhood. Since our only training ground for parenting is in our parents' home, we tend to do it the way we saw it done. If our parents used violence, we likely will perpetuate the same style in the next generation. All Jephthah knew about family was that family members were self-interested, and they rejected members who threatened their self-interest. When he left his family, he also became

When Parents Fail 45

self-interested. The only way he knew to protect his own life was to sacrifice someone else's.

Death from child abuse in our society is often a raging act of self-preservation. How many times do we hear on the news that the cries of a child threatened a parent's sanity? He or she beat the child to death in a senseless effort to gain control, not out of any good intention of making the child behave.

The joy of Jephthah's daughter soon turned to sadness. She submitted to the vow immediately and prepared to mourn her own death. Not once did she challenge the vow. Children readily accept bad parenting and abusive behavior. Their parents are the people who love them. They have to believe that if parents hurt them, it must be for their own good.

Jephthah's daughter not only respected her father's vow, she believed that his battles and his promises would bring honor to God. But after Abraham's aborted sacrifice of Isaac, God does not ask us to make human sacrifices. God asks us to give up only the things that absorb our devotion and draw us away from God. Any discipline that uses God as a threat against children is blasphemous.

A little girl told her teacher each day that her head ached and that her parents were sure she was being punished by God for some sin. They forced her to pray hard and to atone for her sin in order to be healed. Then, by some chance, they discovered that is was not sin at all, but a too-tight ponytail that made the girl's head hurt. How God and children suffer for parents' misuse of faith!

Not every case of child abuse is sinister or completely selfish. Sometimes parents simply make mistakes. Like Jephthah, we say things in the heat of the moment that we regret later. In my first full-time pastorate, the church office was in the parsonage. It was a small room next to the main living area for our family. We had two daughters at the time, ages five and three. This particular morning the inspirational juices were not flowing too well in my study. At the same time I heard voices from the living area that sounded like the youngsters were giving Anna Mary a hard time. After a few minutes I could stand it no longer. In frustration and anger I dashed out of the office, spanked the oldest daughter, and sat her on the stairsteps for five minutes. Quickly I went back into the study. No inspiration for Sunday's sermon made an approach for landing. The only thing on my mind was my unfair action against my daughter. I was not a seasoned parent, but I was developing a sensitivity to little people's feelings. Before the five minutes were up, I found myself kneeling on the steps in front of our daughter saying, "Daddy didn't know why he was spanking you. I did it because I was frustrated. Will you forgive me?" Looking into those beautiful blue, tear-stained eyes, I saw love and forgiveness shining through as she said, "I forgive you, Daddy." That daughter, now an adult, has a vivid, warm memory of that incident. I'm so glad I didn't assume that she was just a child and would soon forget it.

Parents sometimes assume that children will surely understand their bursts of anger and that it will all go away without them making amends. But in parent-child relationships, it is extremely important for mother or father to talk things out and seek forgiveness when they have injured their children emotionally or physically. Children need to know that parents do make mistakes and that love heals. It is important for youngsters to have the opportunity to forgive and trust people again.

Fearing reprisal and even the wrath of God, children and adolescents are frequently scared to tell anyone about the abuse they suffer. Jephthah's young daughter, however, was able to grieve openly. She asked Jephthah for a two month reprieve so that she could wander the mountains with her girlfriends to work through her emotional and psychological hurt. Opportunities for abused persons to tell their stories are very important. Those possibilities are increasing today.

Christian Parenting

Do we as parents make commitments to God and church responsibilities that place our children in jeopardy? When and where do we as teachers, parents, or childcare providers engage in behavior that may be abusive?

A model for good Christian parenting is found in Mark 10:13-16, the story of Jesus accepting the children gladly when the disciples wanted to send them away. Perhaps they believed children were not important to Jesus, or that Jesus was for adults only. Perhaps they thought the Master was too busy to be disturbed and they needed to spare him from these curiosity seekers. Whatever the reason, Jesus rejected it. "Let the little children come to me; do not stop them . . ." (10:14).

To Jesus, children are people worthy of his time. But more than that, a child's wonder, acceptance, adoration, and innocence are the characteristics of the faithful. Before they have a chance to disbelieve, children believe, and unless we find our way back to a childlikeness, we can never know what the realm of God is like. Faith requires that we accept without the need for proof, that we find awe and wonder in the greatness of God, that we praise God, and that we strive for innocence from anger, hate, jealousy, and greed.

Parents are not perfect. Neither are children always innocent. Without a doubt, children need discipline and firm direction. But when discipline begins to damage a child, it becomes abuse. Discipline ought to promote the qualities of faith in children, not drive them out with belts, humiliation, subservience, or neglect. The very things that frustrate us about children and frustrated the disciples are the things for which Jesus had patience and appreciation. We cannot and should not expect anything from children except what God wants them to be.

As has been mentioned in each session, families must communicate to have healthy relationships, whether they are the relationships of children, spouses, or parents and children. Instead of holding in frustration that will make you explode in anger, tell your children that you are frustrated and why. Practice having patience with children. Don't expect them to know what you know or do things the way you do them. Within reason, let them make their own mistakes. Give them chances to do better. Never belittle them. Offer lots of encouragement. Let your children teach you things. Spend time together. As much as possible, laugh together. Honor their privacy and they will come to you. Respect their decisions and they will ask your advice. Trust them to be their own person and they will imitate the kind way you treat people.

Discussion and Action

1. Discuss incidences you know of where people were rejected in your family or congregation. If you have been rejected and are able, discuss your feelings as you remember them.
2. Make a list of the ways people in the group were disciplined as children. Are any of the methods abusive? Which ones promote a life of faith?
3. Taking vows is a serious matter in the Christian community. Are there occasions where breaking vows would be okay? Under what circumstances? Share something you said that you thought you couldn't take back or make up for.

4. Discuss the affirming and the "infirming" of children in your congregation and home.
5. How would you describe the childlikeness that the faithful must exhibit to enter the kingdom of heaven?
6. Based on Jesus' relationship with children, what would you say are the inalienable rights of children? How are they being protected or neglected in your community?
7. Invite someone to talk to your group about the rudiments of conflict resolution in families. Consider sponsoring a short course on conflict resolution for the whole congregation.

8

Passing On Christlike Values to Children
Deuteronomy 6:4-9; 2 Timothy 1:1-14

God's promise to fulfill a plan of grace for the world was first given to the family of Abraham and culminated in the family of Jesus. The plan promised unconditional love, forgiveness, commitment, and peace. Since the time of Abraham, families, more than any institution, have been able to teach children about the promise and give them a hunger to experience it themselves.

Personal Preparation
1. In addition to reading Deuteronomy 6:4-9, use it in your household for devotions. Ask the family to reflect on its meaning. Compare it to Mark 12:29-31.
2. After reading 2 Timothy 1:1-14, think of a gem of wisdom that came from a grandparent that has been a helpful memory for you.
3. Look at the rooms of your house. Note any memorabilia, pictures, or furniture that was handed down to you. What is the value of that keepsake? What important lessons have been handed down to you in life?
4. Ponder who has been the most caring and helpful mentor in shaping your Christian values.

Understanding

The Shema

In scripture, God gives families a special responsibility to nurture their children into faithful adults who will, in turn, train their children in the faith. Today, as then, Christian values of respect, justice, trust, faith, hope, and love are passed on to the next generation by example and by intention. These are also the central values of family life. As youth grow in faith, they bring strengths to their own family setting and to the problems that arise.

While family is central to God's promise, God did not define family according to a structure, especially not the traditional, modern family made up of a mother, father, two and a half children, and a two car garage in the suburbs. Family is defined more clearly in scripture as a relationship between people. Biblical families had single parents, adoptive parents, guardians, monogamous families, polygamous families, extended families, and almost every combination of adults and children living in a household, much like today. The thing that held families together was a commitment to faith and a love for one another.

How do we help children want to be people of faith? It is easy to see why children long to belong to a family. Families provide necessities, such as food, shelter, and clothing. They also provide emotional necessities, such as love and appreciation. But what about faith? How do they learn that a relationship with God is as necessary as daily bread? The scriptures of this study provide suggestions for conveying faith through the family from one generation to another. We look first at Deuteronomy 6:4-9, which is also called the Shema from the first word of the text, "Hear."

Deuteronomy claims to be Moses' farewell address to the people of Israel, who were ready to leave the plains of Moab and move into Canaan (their twenty-first century!). Moses would not be going with them to Canaan, but he tells them in Deuteronomy 6:1-3 what they need to know, particularly that they must love and revere God as they move into the promised land. To their questions of why, why do we and our children and our children's children need to revere God, Moses encourages them, saying: If you do these things, "you and your children and your children's children may fear the Lord your God all the days of your life, . . . your days may be long [For the Hebrews at this time the reward for obedience to God was not immortality, but prolonged life.], . . . it may go well with you [that life will be filled with joy and meaning] . . . . so that you may multiply greatly."

To remember this most important lesson, Moses commands them to repeat over and over the words of the Shema (Deut. 6:4-5). The Shema is a famous teaching tool to keep before us the most important lesson of our lives. And Moses gives this responsibility to families: "Recite [these words] to your children and talk about them when you are at home and when you are away, when you lie down and when your rise. Bind them as a sign on your hand, fix them as an emblem on your forehead, and write them on the doorposts of your house and on your gates" (6:7-9).

When You Lie Down and When You Rise

Moses makes the routine and the discipline of saying the words almost as important as the words themselves. It is through the repetition that the words become part of us, a sort of second nature, the first thing we think of when someone asks if we believe in God. Interestingly, it is not in the temple or the church that we should become accustomed to saying the words, but in the ordinary places of our lives, such as the bedroom and the doorway. These are the places where we are together as family and where the words of the Shema make the most sense.

The routine depends first on parents keeping their own faith alive and aflame. Shifting the responsibility to grandparents or the village priest is not adequate. Be sure to love God yourself with everything you have—heart, soul, might. Demonstrate a working faith to your children. If you are consistent in the way you talk about faith and the way you live it out, they will be interested.

We are not limited to saying the Shema in just one place. Moses makes it easy for modern families as well to educate their children about faith, even when they're on the move. Talk about the words when you are at home and when you are away. Family vacations are not a vacation from the disciplines of faith and remembering God.

Our oldest granddaughter wanted to visit us by herself from the time she was three. Since her family lived eight hundred miles from us, we made long trips by car to pick her up or take her home. When traveling got boring for Japhia, Anna Mary would tell stories from her own girlhood. She told anecdotes from Sunday School, times her mother settled sibling squabbles, breakfast on the farm with eight children squirming while Dad read the scripture and prayed. There were narrations about Japhia's mother's incessant questioning, her attempts to ride a bike, and family events. After each story, Japhia would say, "Tell it again, Grandma," or "Tell another story, Grandma." For many summers, the request for stories continued, and values and faith were transmitted along the way.

The Hebrews kept the word of the Shema in places where they would see them often. "Bind them as a sign on your hand, fix them as an emblem on your forehead." Christian homes should display symbols of the faith and the Bible to constantly remind families of God's instruction. Mustard seeds, prayer cards, crosses, and rainbows are common reminders of faith.

"And write them on the doorposts of your house and on your gates." Have something more than a welcome mat at the entrance to your house. Place some symbols at the door that will tell your children and friends that God is not only in the holy temple but also in your house.

The Psalter (the Hebrew hymnal) is a chant that indicates the importance of teaching and modeling faith in the family. At one place it says, "We will not hide them [teachings] from their children; we will tell to the coming generation the glorious deeds of the Lord, and his might, and the wonders that he has done" (Psa. 78:4). It reminds me of the tune and the words of a hymn sung in my boyhood congregation about the importance of God's word.

> Sing them over again to me,
> Wonderful words of life.
> Let me more of their beauty see,
> Wonderful words of life.

Eunice to Lois to Timothy

Repetition of the Shema is one way to pass along the faith to children in families. Another way for families to train children is an emerging popular method today called mentoring—see 2 Timothy 1:1-14. Timothy testifies to the effect that religious family rituals and faith sharing had upon his faith development and, finally, his work in the church.

Paul appears to think of himself as Timothy's spiritual mentor. He refers to him as "my beloved child" (2 Tim. 1:2), which means my true child in the faith. He affirms Timothy, thanking God for him, his faith, and his growth (1:3-4). But Timothy's first mentors were his mother and his grandmother. Through the thoughtfulness and love of his mother, Lois, and his grandmother, Eunice, Timothy's faith began in the home. We know little more than that about his home life except that his mother was Jewish and his father was Greek (Acts 16:1). His family is another example of the wide variety of families in the Bible who are people of faith, but who defy a standard definition of a healthy family.

Whatever the situation may have been in this religiously mixed marriage, Timothy's parents accepted the special God-given responsibility to families to nurture their children into faithful adults. Faith in God was transmitted through Timothy's family for three generations (2 Tim. 1:5). Additional support for that nurturing process in his family is confirmed in 2 Timothy 3:15, "And how from childhood you have known the sacred writings that are able to instruct you for salvation through faith in Christ Jesus."

Some years ago I became friends of a unique older couple living in my community. The wife was a matriarchal type from a southern pentecostal congregation, Bible-believing, dyed-in-the-wool believer in Jesus Christ. The husband, an excellent chef, was a calm, mystical, Italian Roman Catholic. At that time they had custody of two grandchildren whose parents deserted them. From that diverse family setting, family rituals of prayer, meditation, Bible reading, and daily family time were regularly observed. It was gratifying to see the values of respect, trust, obedience, love, joy, and faith in God transmitted into the lives of those granddaughters as they moved into their teens.

Like Timothy, children learn what they live, and the home is a child's first classroom for learning about God and others. Parents are the first and most influential teachers or mentors whether they plan to be or not. Children imitate whatever behavior and reason they observe. Christian families can be more intentional about their role as mentors and convey what needs to be learned rather than passively imparting their own habits and beliefs.

Many church families are using mentoring programs in the congregation to encourage and train young people in the way of faith. A mature Christian adult is enlisted or chosen by a youth to be a mentor. The two partners strike a covenant that calls for spending time together in experiences that build faith. Lavon Welty, author of *Side by Side: Mentoring Guide for Congregational Youth* (Faith & Life Press), lays out one program for youth and mentoring adults to use in congregations.

Learning Christlike values and becoming a person of faith is difficult today. Young people have lots of commitments and many temptations. To many of them, Christianity seems hypocritical or irrelevant or "uncool." Moreover, as disciples of Christ, many of us get discouraged about the lack of spiritual growth in our families. We know how slowly Christian faith influences culture. We feel inadequate for the task of mentoring young people. It's then we must remember Paul's words: "For this reason I remind you to rekindle the gift of God that is within you" (1:6). After all, our victories or failures do not bring honor or disgrace to us, but to God.

Guidelines

These are my convictions about how families educate children for faith:

1. Maintaining the health and well-being of our children is primarily the responsibility of parents. As Christian parents we also have the serious commitment to foster the spiritual lives of our children.
2. Faith formation is an ongoing process by which families, especially parents, witness and demonstrate their faith to their children.
3. The church was intended to be a gathering place for families, not a substitute for the religious education in the home.
4. The family is to be a laboratory for soul work.

As you define how your family will remember God, make your own list of convictions. Keep it next to the Great Commandment by your doorpost, on your garden gate, in the phone book, the bedroom, and at the kitchen sink.

Discussion and Action

1. Talk about your faith development in your family. What affected you most? What resources, symbols, family events, and rituals were meaningful?
2. Congregations spend a lot of time discussing the appropriate symbols for worship in chapels and sanctuaries. What symbols do you intentionally place in your household to express the Christian faith and values? Consider making some kind of mezuzah to hold a copy of the Shema.
3. Debate the statement that the church was intended to be a gathering place for families, not a substitute for religious education in the home.

4. Spiritual mentoring is a popular innovation in the church. Consider the merits of this approach. For whom? At what age? Can we actually teach faith "into" children? How? Does your congregation have a mentoring program? Talk to the pastor or youth pastor about setting one up.
5. To assist parents of young children in passing on faith values, explore with your congregation's education committee a plan for hosting four Sunday morning seminars on Passing On Christlike Values to Children.

9

Changes in Family Life
Ruth 4:13-17; Luke 8:19-21
John 19:25-27

Families only have to take a family portrait to find out how much change they endure over time. A picture taken on any given day represents a family only for a short time. Within months, everyone has grown, aged, married, had children, or passed away. This session looks at how transition affects families and how faith helps families survive transition.

Personal Preparation

1. Read the passages from Ruth and Luke. Note the amount of change Ruth's and Jesus' families endured. Jot down the major transitions in your own life.
2. How does your family handle change? Is it difficult? Is it a joy? What kinds of traditions does your family have to create stability, such as family reunions and holiday meals?
3. This week, ask the following people what family means to them and how they survived a major transition: a person whose mate was called away for military service, an elderly person whose lifelong partner became seriously ill, a child of divorced parents, a divorced person, a person with a permanent disability.

Understanding

In my reading I learned of two men who lived in a houseboat that was permanently docked in a marina. One night while they slept a storm came up. The boat broke from its moorings and drifted out to sea. Next morning one of the men got up early and went out on the deck. He could hardly believe what he saw. Rousing his friend he cried, "Wake up! Wake up! We're not here anymore!"

That's life. From week to week, things are not what they used to be. The only thing we can count on is change. Some changes come naturally. They are part of life's passages, such as conception, birth, infancy, childhood, adolescence, adulthood, death. Other changes happen because of choices we make, such as going to college, changing vocations, choosing to sin. Still other shifts come because of the decisions others make that affect us, such as the decision to desert a marriage, driving drunk, changing company policy. Changes affect families, but families can also affect the way we handle change. Families of faith, such as Ruth's and Jesus' families, whose foundation is a trust in the unconditional grace of God, survive change well and use it for good.

Resisting change and transition in life is a miserable and long-standing argument with the inevitable. King Saul tried to hang onto the kingship long after the people needed a change in leadership. Ezra grieved over the changes in Judah that happened while the Israelites were in exile. Herod saw the birth of Jesus as a sign of great change encroaching on his comfortable setup as king. Each tried to preserve the past. Not only did they lose the past, they could not be part of the future, either.

Everything that God has done has required change. God cleansed the world with a flood and required a new life. God turned barren women into mothers. God changed slaves to free people. God gave us Jesus who would stand the world on its head. Faith is a change from old ways to new, a change from death to life.

Ruth

Many Bible families symbolize the acceptance of change and promise that comes from transition even when it is difficult or painful. Who more than Ruth experienced change in her life and her family, and who more than she, used change for good? Because of her transition and her great faith, she became the ancestor of Jesus.

In four short chapters Ruth faced about every upheaval imaginable. She grew up in a Moabite home, but married a Judahite named Chilion. The two cultures blended in this marriage were antagonistic on matters of faith. While Moabites traced their ancestry to Lot, the nephew of Abraham, they were not monotheistic like the Israelites. The chief Moabite god, Chemosh, ruled over many lesser gods, whom Ruth would be required to forsake when she converted to her mother-in-law's faith.

Before she could become a mother, Ruth was widowed, as were her sister-in-law and mother-in-law. In addition to grieving, the women had to face the harsh conditions of being women without means of support—no children, no husbands, no brothers-in-law to fulfill marital obligations. She could have returned to her birth family, but she chose instead to emigrate with her mother-in-law to Judah, a place that would not treat a foreigner well nor extend her any rights.

In her pledge to stick by her mother-in-law, Ruth agreed to convert her religion to Judaism. By default perhaps, Ruth faced a future caring for her aging mother-in-law and living in an extended family with three generations eventually under one roof. She remarried for safety and financial security (perhaps also for love) and gave birth to a child who would be an important link to the family of Jesus.

How did Ruth endure cross-cultural marriage, widowhood, poverty, emigration, remarriage, birth, an extended family household, and eldercare? In part, she survived by creating a family, not just to secure herself or make things stop changing, but to pledge love and support even in hard times. Family does not ensure good times, but it can be a source of love and grace in hard times. Building a family is an action of faith and hope. And perpetuation of the generations is a confession that God has indeed made life meaningful and worth living. Out of hardship and grief, Ruth could still say that life was good.

Like Ruth, Mary Harris Jones was a woman who knew tremendous grief and transition. Born in Ireland, she and her husband and children emigrated to the United States where he worked as an iron molder. But he and their children perished in an epidemic soon after their move to Tennessee. Then Mary moved to Chicago where, sometime later, she lost all her possessions in the Chicago fire. After her family was decimated and her home ruined, Mary Jones made a "family" of the poor laborers in her community and worked tirelessly for safety and security for families in mines, factories, and slums. Everyone knew her as Mother Jones, a woman whose faith could not be shaken and who inspired families to hope and faith.

The Family of Jesus

It could not have been easy to be a member of the family of Jesus or to live through the anguished transitions of their lives. Little did Mary know when the angel announced she would be the mother of the Savior that Jesus would be despised and misunderstood. It was not likely that she was prepared for some of his teachings about family. If she knew what life had in store, would she have had the courage to try it? Would we?

Perhaps one of the most difficult things families face is a child's rejection. Though rebellion and independence are natural for children, families never stop longing to be loved by the ones they love so much. It must have been painful for Mary when Jesus ignored her and said, "My mother and my brothers are those who hear the word of God and do it" (Luke 8:21). On other occasions he advised giving up all attachments and obligations to family, even burial, to be able to devote everything to God.

Mary also must have bemoaned the serious trouble with the authorities that Jesus faced. She is like the parent who wants to keep her child out of trouble but cannot, and is finally resigned to the possibility that the child will be imprisoned, hurt, or even killed. Many families of troubled children can neither successfully live with the child, nor sever ties completely. They try and they try to work things out, but sometimes it's just not possible.

Jesus could not be contained within Mary's family either. He was part of a greater family. His words of rejection sound harsh, but taken another way, they are words that embrace the world as family. We, too, must widen our view of family to our church, our community, and our friends. We share with them an intimacy and connectedness that holds us up in times of trouble. When children are in trouble or marriage partners separate or conflict threatens a single family, it is the wider community that plays the role of family, the people who will always be there for us.

Jesus was not *unmindful* of Mary. Even from the cross he commended her into the care of another son (John 19:25-27). The new son was Jesus' beloved disciple. This disciple could provide for Mary after Jesus' death.

Extended Family

As congregations, we could do better at comforting people who go through difficult life passages. We do well in a crisis, such as a death or a funeral, but in the weeks and months that follow, when people face the hard work of putting their lives together, we have to stick with them as brothers and sisters, helping them through a transition.

In my own life, I am trying to go the long haul with friends who have lost family members through death. Not long ago, I was thinking about Oscar whose wife had died of cancer four weeks earlier. That evening before choir rehearsal I saw him standing by himself. Approaching him I said, "Oscar, I was thinking about you this week." In my mind I was thinking, I wonder how Oscar feels walking into an empty house when he comes home from work? Immediately Oscar unloaded all his stored up hurt and let me share the load of his grief.

Jesus has given us all an assignment to be beloved disciples, helping each other through changes in Christlike ways. At the very least, we can be a listening ear for members of our family and for members of the church family. Letting people reason out loud or unload a hidden hurt, as Oscar did, may be all they need to make it through troublesome transitions in life.

When transitions are tougher, some people may need a friend or relative to intervene and provide real assistance. Changes can leave people confused or unable to think clearly. As caring friends or relatives, we may need to step in and advise them how to deal with a transition or urge them to get professional counseling for problems, such as delinquent children, abusive spouses, aged parents, or terminal illnesses. The trick is knowing when to listen, when to confront, and when to call in a professional. As "beloved disciples" who truly care about friends and relatives, we should know the limits of what we can do for someone else. Sometimes we are the best help when we know the time to ask for someone else's help.

As disciples to each other, we can face crises and changes because we already have deep relationships on which to draw. When change comes, as it inevitably will, the engine of love and support that has driven our families and friendships all along goes into high gear. But when there is a breakdown in the family, transition is more difficult. That is why it is so important to work on communication, respect, trust, and all the family values every day with the people nearest you. The smooth running engine will more likely run well in poor conditions than the engine held together with baling wire and coat hangers.

Unhealthy families may not survive transition. A young white woman fell in love with a black student at college. When she told her parents that she wanted to marry her boyfriend, the parents refused to support a mixed race marriage. When she went ahead with plans to marry him, they cut off all communication with their daughter. The ones to step in as surrogate parents to the young woman and her boyfriend were an older couple in the community who used their retirement to provide a ministry to college students. Each week they hosted as many as a hundred college students in their home for a meal. And kept up with students' birthdays, graduations, job searches, struggles and pains. They stood up with the couple at their wedding and stayed in touch as parents and children forever after.

A true family is made up of the people who come through in crises and changes because they have also been there for the little day-to-day joys and struggles of being a family.

Discussion and Action

1. Share some of the major transitions in your lives. How does your family handle transition?
2. How can families who blend religions, races, ages, and ethnicities prepare for the changes they will face?
3. Who do you find more helpful during transition? Your family? Or people outside the family, such as friends or church family? Why?
4. How are you and your church family keeping in touch with families who are in transition, such as people away serving missions, the unemployed, those who have had a death in the family, or the elderly who are bedridden or limited in movement?
5. Work together to come up with guidelines for knowing when to refer a friend or family member to professional help. Make up a list of names and phone numbers of people and agencies that can help. Type the list and make it available to people in your church.
6. Practice active listening skills that will help you be a better listener. Find a partner. Let one partner use two or three minutes to tell the other partner about a frustration in his or her family. At the end of the time limit, have the listening partners summarize the story as they heard them. The person who told the story should correct any misconceptions and clarify any details not covered in the summary. Switch roles and repeat several times with different partners.

10

The Family of God
Ephesians 4:1-6, 11-16
1 John 3:1-2; 5:1-5

No matter how our blood-related or adopted families are configured, we can always count on belonging to the family of God. Of course, the members of God's family have their bad moments just like our personal families. But God, the faultless, forgiving parent, holds the family together and desires that we know the joy of living as true brothers and sisters.

Personal Preparation

1. Read Ephesians 4:1-6, 11-16 and 1 John 3:1-2; 5:1-5. After reading these passages, how would you define the family of God?
2. Who, in your understanding, is part of the family of God? Do you feel as though you belong? Why or why not?
3. How is your congregation like a family? What are its weaknesses and its strengths? Is it superior to your personal family in some way? How?

Understanding

How many times have you heard someone say something is "cool" or "really, really, really, really phat" (the newest lingo for great). The more we use an expression, the less punch it packs. It's only when we hold certain words in reserve for special occasions that they have any real impact on the hearer.

The church is just as guilty as anyone of overusing words and phrases. Ideas that should be brimming with meaning begin to sound jingoistic and not very sincere. We say that we all belong to the family of God and that we are children of God. We like the warm feeling we get when we say that regardless of race, religion, and biological family structure, we are all God's children. But do we truly believe it and make others feel they are part of the family, too?

The meaning of these sayings is dulled by overuse. Recently I was listening to the chaplain at a retirement village say a prayer: "Lord, we do not only pray for ourselves, but we pray for your guidance of all your children in the world." Who was he praying for? Who are God's children? Who is included in the family of God? Are we God's children automatically?

Family: Created in God's Image

During this session we will look at three definitions or understandings of the family of God in the scriptures. The most obvious and most inclusive idea of family comes from the account of creation. According to Genesis, all people belong to the Creator's family because "God created humankind in his image" (Gen. 1:27). Into the nostrils of humankind God breathed the breath of life (Gen. 2:7). Prophet Isaiah also included every person in the family of God when he said, "Thus says God, the Lord, who created the heavens and stretched them out, who spread out the earth and what comes from it, who gives breath to the people upon it and spirit to those who walk in it" (Isa. 42:5).

Paul is another proponent of the whole family of God. "From one ancestor [God] made all nations to inhabit the whole earth, and he allotted the times of their existence and the boundaries of the places where they would live, so that they would search for God and perhaps grope for him and find him—though indeed he is not far from each one of us. For 'In him we live and move and have our being'" (Acts 17:26-28). All human beings are in God's family because of God's gift of life and personhood.

I find it exciting to relate to people by trying to see them as people first, free from labels others have put on them. That's what I see Jesus doing. He initially disregarded the judgments on people and looked at them as individuals first. Only after that did he seek to offer healing, help, and hope.

Looking into the eyes of people who are rebuffed because of divorce, misunderstood by Christians because they are successful in business, mistrusted because they are church, community, or political leaders, dismissed because they are fundamentalist Christians, and seeing them as people first, lets me look past the characteristics that we have put on each other and see the person that God has created as part of the family. I sense a kinship with all others based on merely being human, devoid of all labels, created in the image of God.

The Family of Believers

Then there is another way to think of the family of God. It is also biblical. It comes out of the tragedy of disobedience of the human race toward the Creator. Because of the sin of self-centeredness and self-will, humankind turned away from the Lord. So Jehovah God sought out a family of people who were responsive to the call and guidance of one God. God called Abraham to make a family for God. So Abraham became the ancestor of a family that lived out a monotheistic faith in God.

The Lord said to Abraham, "I will make of you a great nation, and I will bless you, and make your name great, so that you will be a blessing" (Gen. 12:1). This covenant is repeated numerous times in the Old Testament, as in Isaiah 42:6. "I am the Lord, I have called you in righteousness, I have taken you by the hand and kept you; I have given you as a covenant to the people, a light to the nations." In response to God's blessing, people who worship God are members of the family. This understanding of the family of God puts limits on the notion that everyone is a member of the family by virtue of being human. It is for those who believe in and express faith in one God.

We saw in the last session that Jesus loved everyone, but he gave special invitations to the family of God, to those who believed (Matt. 12:46-50). His mother and brothers wanted to talk to Jesus but they could not get through the crowd. Someone told Jesus his family was trying to make their way to him, but he replied, " 'Who is my mother, and who are my brothers?' And pointing to his disciples, he said, 'Here are my mother and my brothers! For whoever does the will of my Father in heaven is my brother and sister and mother.' " This is not a method for weeding out the people we don't like, however. If we were to look at the list of people in the Gospels who understood who Jesus was or who believed he was the Son of God, we would not see the religious leaders and the upright people in the community. These were the outcasts: tax collectors, prostitutes, and lepers.

Jesus was not denying the importance of bloodline families. He was saying, however, that the family of God is bound together by the bonds of spirit, not those of blood. There is a kinship of common commitment and obedience to God that is undeniably strong and binding. This kind of belonging comes by choice.

The Covenant Family - Volunteer

This brings us to a third understanding of the family of God. Through the arrival of Jesus—his teachings, his death, and his resurrection—came an expanded understanding of God and God's covenant. The followers of Jesus became the extension of God's promise to Abraham, and the New Testament church became God's covenant people who shall "be a light to all the nations."

We are not members of God's family by virtue of being human or by simply believing. It is by virtue of becoming part of the new covenant, the church, that qualifies us for becoming members of the family of God in the truest sense. With excitement Apostle Paul said he was giving his life for this, "to make everyone see what is the plan of the mystery hidden for ages in God who created all things, so that through the church the wisdom of God in its rich variety might now be made known. . . . For this reason I bow my knees before the Father, from whom every family in heaven and on earth takes its name" (Eph. 3:9-15). For Jew and Gentile, slave and free, male and female, the church was to be like a family for families.

The Church as Family

New Testament writers use several images to describe the family of God. Paul compares the church family to a human body. The church is the body of Christ, Paul said. Christ is the head. Believers in Christ are the parts of the body. Each member has its function. Each receives its spiritual impulses and directives from the head, Jesus. Under the impulses of Jesus, the body functions in an attitude of unity.

In Ephesians 4 Paul enlarges this metaphor, saying that unity in the church family develops when we recognize the gifts of each member and the goal toward which each gift is to be used. The church family is to organize and call persons to use their gifts . . .

- to help members and families in the congregation to develop stability in Christlike living,

- to encourage individuals and families to avoid tearing down healthy family life,
- to help individuals and families develop communication skills for honest confrontation and dialogue. (See Ephesians 4:7-16.)

The Dysfunctional Church Family

According to 1 John 3:1-2; 4:7-12; and 5:1-5, those who love God will love one another, because to love God is to keep the commandments and the greatest thing that God commands is that we love God and neighbor. This is one of those things we espouse easily, but do poorly.

With all the struggles in congregations today, we have to wonder if the family of God is actually dysfunctional at times. Like the Corinthian church, we fight over who has the right interpretation of things, who should lead, who is acting inappropriately, and who can take part in what. All families have disagreements; it's how we work through them that is the barometer of congregational health. If groups can disagree but still respect and honor each other, they have health.

Like families, we should tolerate some variety in the views and interpretations of church members. The views of "sibling rivals" in the church can complement each other, just as Mary and Martha together provided all that Jesus needed. When people in the congregation get tired of announcements from the social justice committee on Sunday morning or constant pleas from the finance committee or the witness of a spiritual life enthusiast, as though those facets of congregational life were each the most central, they must remember that a congregation without each of these is lacking.

Church families also need boundaries. We easily become "unfaithful" to the church when other more glamorous opportunities come along and woo us away from our primary family, the church. Being more certain about our boundaries would help us be more committed to the church. Boundaries would also help us to stop abusing people in the church, especially pastors who are buffeted around by unruly congregations. One pastor tried, to no avail, to get his congregation to understand that he was there to "prophesy," teach, and visit, but that he was not the slave of the congregation who would do everything from janitorial services to staffing the nursery. Some congregations like to hire someone to do their work while they sit back and enjoy the program on Sunday morning.

The church is dysfunctional when it is the cause of pain and brokenness in the family of God, but it is doing what it is supposed to do when it is the place where pain and brokenness are healed. My church used to practice "avoidance" or what others called the "ban." When members of the church violated the practices and ordinances of the church, congregations would discipline them and try to bring the offending members to repentance by avoiding contact with them until they saw the error of their ways.

When it worked, the ban successfully admonished a member and strengthened the whole group. Many times, however, the ban was vindictive and punitive. It occasionally condemned innocent people or made monumental problems out of seemingly trivial offenses.

In very recent times, a congregation banned a person who owed them money. They did not exclude the person; rather they assigned someone to be with him each day, though no one was permitted to talk to him. He was kept in the community while he was being disciplined so that they could demonstrate their love for him and their interest in his repentance. He had been arrested and spent time in mental institutions, but said he preferred the ban. Society had looked at him as a crazy person and locked him up, but the church took him in and worked with him.

An historic leader in my denomination once said that the congregation was far more interested in taking back a disciplined member than they were in expelling her. Facing our brokenness is difficult. No one likes conflict. But the healing that happens when we confront caringly makes for a stronger family.

The Healthy Church Family

Every dimension of healthy families that we have talked about in these sessions applies to the healthy church family, and more so. Values of trust, respect, open communication, and appreciation make for a healthy church family as well as for the biological family. The church is a single-parent family with God as the sole head. Congregations can heal brokenness, help brothers and sisters get along, establish and respect boundaries, pass on Christlike values to children, and help ease transitions in congregational life.

The characteristics of family apply to the church even more, because the church is a family by choice. It is the group that comes together because it wants to glorify God. And nothing gives more honor to God than treating God and each other with compassion.

Individual families are the result of fate, but the church has purpose. The people in the church want to work together.

But the difference that ultimately makes the church family the supreme family is that our parent, God, will not let us go. When we fail as a family in our personal lives or in the life of the church, God is tough and God is forgiving. We can neglect God and even offend God, but we cannot go away from God. If Hosea can take back his unfaithful wife and treat her children as his own, how much more does our God take back the church and its failures and treat us as beloved, rebellious children.

Discussion and Action

1. Compare your definitions of the family of God. How are they alike? different?
2. Review the three biblical understandings of God's family. Then raise these questions. Can you agree with each definition or only one? Which do you agree with most? Which ones create the most uncertainty for you? The most tension?
3. Talk about the ways in which your congregation or covenant group is like a family. What are its family strengths and weaknesses?
4. What attitudes or issues divide the family of God locally, globally, or ecumenically? How do these issues affect you?
5. Have you chosen your church family? Were you born into it? What can you do in a chosen family that you cannot do in a family you inherit?
6. Communication was mentioned in almost every session as a necessary element of healthy families. How would you rate the communication in your family? What would improve the communication in your family?
7. Review the family values listed in the first lesson. Talk about what you've learned.

Suggestions for Sharing and Prayer

This material is designed for covenant groups that spend an hour in sharing and praying together, in addition to the hour of Bible study. These suggestions will help to relate the group's sharing to their study of *Real Families: From Patriarchs to Prime Time*. Session-by-session ideas are given, followed by general resources. This guide was compiled by Harriet and Ronald Finney of North Manchester, Indiana. They are Church of the Brethren General Board staff for Family Ministry.

1. Values and Strengths in Family Life

- Describe to your covenant group an experience of nurturing within your childhood family. Was that experience common for you in your growing-up years? Or was it an isolated incident? Was it part of a family tradition that has repeated itself over several generations?

- What are the important values within your family? How does your family live them out?

- Have any of the families represented in your covenant group found effective ways to have a family devotional time? Share ideas that have worked. If you have not established a devotional time in your family, consider how you might begin. One new resource, edited by Susan Vogt, is entitled: *Just Family Nights: 60 Activities to Keep Your Family Together in a World Falling Apart* (Brethren Press, Elgin, IL, 1994, 800-441-3712).

- Reflect on the family in which Jesus grew up. Sing together "Away in a Manger." Then use the hymn "O Little Town of Bethlehem" to begin a time of prayer.

- Mention any prayer requests or thanksgivings from the families represented in your covenant group; have a time of prayer for each of those families. Agree to pray daily for one another throughout this ten-week study.

- As a closing prayer, read together or sing the words of the hymn "Help Us to Help Each Other" (p. 80).

2. Living as Singles

- ❑ Describe how you moved away from your parents' home. Did you leave abruptly, or was it a gradual transition? Were you "pushed out of the nest," or were you eager to leave? Were you single or married at the time? What were your feelings? the feelings of others in the family? Did you ever move back home again? What was that like?

- ❑ Have each person draw a twelve-inch circle on a piece of paper and divide it into six pieces like a pie. Label each piece this way:

  a. things I like to ponder

  b. work I enjoy

  c. free time activities

  d. places I find God

  e. gifts God has given to me

  f. important people in my life

  List your responses in each area. Then discuss the chart with your group. Be sure to mention the things that give you a sense of wholeness and affirmation as an individual.

- ❑ Intimacy (closeness) with God is possible through prayer and meditation. Teresa of Avila was a Carmelite nun who lived from 1515-1582. She wrote of intimacy with God in "Spiritual Espousal" (pp. 76-77). How do you respond to this description of intimacy with God in terms of the marriage relationship? Does it remind you of Ephesians 5:25-31, in which Paul compares a marriage relationship to Christ and the church? What images or analogies would you use to describe an intimate relationship with God?

- ❑ Tell about times when you have felt especially close to God. What has enabled you to be close to God? As a group, read the words of hymns or prayers that express this nearness to God. Some examples are "Jesus, Lover of My Soul," "Jesus, My Lord, My God, My All," "Love Divine, All Loves Excelling," "I Am Thine, O Lord." Look in your hymnal to find others. Spend some time in prayer for each other.

- ❑ Sing together the hymn "Help Us to Help Each Other" as a closing prayer.

3. Single-Parent Families

- Write five "I wonder . . ." statements related to single-parent families, for example: I wonder how it feels to be a child and lose a parent, I wonder if people want to hear my story of what happened, I wonder if single-parent families feel support in my congregation.

- Is there a way in which your covenant group can respond to the "wondering" questions you have raised? What does your congregation already do to minister to single-parent families in ways that offer hope and tangible support?

- Pray for single-parent families. Think about ways in which to put your prayer into action, for example: including them in some of your family outings, offering friendship and a "listening ear," spending time with the children in the family.

- Share traditions or ideas for families that strengthen families, regardless of the shape of that family.

- In closing, sing together "Help Us to Help Each Other," noticing in particular the words to verses 1 and 2.

4. Pain and Brokenness in Family Relationships

- As a group read a scripture or sing a hymn that expresses words of healing and comfort, such as Psalm 40:1-3; Psalm 46; Isaiah 49:14-15; "O Healing River" (p. 81); "Precious Lord, Take My Hand"; "What a Friend We Have in Jesus." Find other verses and hymns to share with the group.

- Reflect on the pain and brokenness you have experienced in your own family or in families you care about. In a prayerful attitude, share these concerns with your covenant group. After each concern say as a group, "Bring healing to our lives, O God." For example, a group member might say, "My mother and my sister can't be together without arguing about something." And the group may respond: "Bring healing to their lives, O God."

- Pray together this prayer for reconciliation:

    Lord, our God,
      great, eternal, wonderful,
      utterly to be trusted:
         you give life to us all,

> you help those who come to you,
> you give hope to those who cry to you.
>
> Forgive our sins, secret and open,
> and rid us of every habit of thought
> that stands against the gospel.
>
> Set our hearts at peace,
> so we may live our lives before you
> confidently and without fear,
> through Jesus Christ, our Lord. AMEN
>
> <div align="right">From <i>Hymnal: A Worship Book.</i> Copyright © 1992 Brethren Press, Elgin, IL;
Faith and Life Press, Newton, KS; Mennonite Publishing House, Scottdale, PA.</div>

- In closing this session, have a pitcher of water and a basin and towel on a table before the group. Think of the areas in your family that need healing, pour water over one another's hands to symbolize the cleansing and healing of water in our lives. Close with a group prayer or by singing "O Healing River" or "Help Us to Help Each Other."

5. Brothers, Sisters, Siblings

- Tell a funny story about you and your siblings growing up.
- Do you and your brothers and sisters all tell the same stories about growing up? In what ways do you feel differently about some of the same events? Why do you think that is so?
- Pray aloud or silently, first confessing things that make you angry with a sibling. Then offer sentence prayers telling what you can appreciate about the same sibling and asking for reconciliation.
- Tell how your family receives and shows God's grace and redemption.
- Pray together for forgiveness, and affirm God's faithfulness. Conclude the prayer with Psalm 103:8-12 or John 3:16-17. Work in pairs to memorize portions or all of these passages. Say them together from memory.
- Close your group time by singing prayerfully "Help Us to Help Each Other."

6. Respecting Boundaries

- What boundaries exist in your family?
  a. related to privacy
  b. related to possessions
  c. related to covenants/agreements
  d. related to sex
  e. other

  Jot down your responses in each case and compare with the rest of the group.

- What boundaries of time, space, or behavior do you need or want in your life that you do not currently have? How can you move toward positive change in this area?

- In their book *Living, Loving, Leading,* David and Karen Mains use the term "mental fidelity." By that they mean being faithful to one's spouse in their fantasies and daydreams, as well as in their actions. What do you think the boundaries should be between marriage partners who are faithful to each other? What did Jesus mean in Matthew 5:28?

- Read the words together, or sing the hymn "When Love Is Found," by Brian Wren (pp. 82-83).

- Use Psalm 51 as a prayer to be read aloud by your covenant group. This is a psalm of David, prayed after the prophet Nathan was sent by God to remind him of the boundaries he crossed in his relationship with Bathsheba.

- Close your time together by singing "Help Us to Help Each Other."

7. When Parents Fail

- Name cases of violence against parents or children that are in the news these days. Then think of all the cases of violence against children or parents in the Bible. Talk about how things have changed or stayed the same. Pray aloud for insight on how to reduce violence in families.

- Lift up the resources or agencies available in your community to assist parents in the task of raising the children. Make a list and, if you can, tell a success story about each organization in its work with families.

- Young children use their entire bodies in the activities in which they engage. Create a prayer that could be taught to a young child, including body movement and symbolic gestures. Repeat this prayer several times around the circle of your group. Plan to teach it to a child. For example, try this intercessory prayer:
  a. Stand with arms extended in front of you, and palms up. Name a person for whom you want to pray.
  b. Slowly raise your arms upward, palms still up, as you visualize the person whose name has been lifted up to God.
  c. Turn palms down, and slowly lower your arms, now visualizing the person being prayed for, receiving God's blessing upon their head.
  d. Repeat the prayer, naming another person to pray for.

  Encourage members of the group to create their own "body prayers" and teach them to children.

- Can you remember a time as a child when your parents or another adult praised you? What was that experience like? What are some ways that you can praise children and encourage them in their discipleship?

- Pray responsively as a group the "Prayer of Intercession" (pp.77-78) or the "Prayer of Confession" and "Assurance of Pardon" (pp. 78-79).

- Sing "Help Us to Help Each Other," thinking especially of ways in which we can help parents and children in our church and community.

8. Passing on Christlike Values to Children

- What is your first memory of Jesus? Did it come from your family, church, or some specific occasion? Who were the people who influenced you to become an active member of the church? What can you do to encourage children in the church? Together, think up a Christian rite of passage for children, moving from a simple faith to a more adult faith and commitments to the church.

- Who taught you to pray? How are your prayers as an adult different from your childhood prayers? How are they similar?

Suggestions for Sharing and Prayer 75

- What values would you especially like to pass on to children in your family and church? How will you do that? Examples include writing a letter, talking with them, taking them on a field trip.
- Plan a time for intergenerational storytelling in your family and church. Share stories in small groups: about your church when you were a child, about how you learned and grew in your faith understanding, about your baptism.
- Put your prayers into action. Plan to participate in a Christian service project as families. (If you are a family of one, join with others.) Some examples include visiting a nursing home, helping to prepare and serve a meal in a homeless shelter, volunteering for a disaster response.
- Close with the hymn "Help Us to Help Each Other," especially verse 3.

9. Changes in Family Life

- Families experience both positive and negative change. Share with the group changes occurring in your family within the past year. How has your family adjusted to those changes?
- What cultures, races, or religions are blended in your family? How has this enriched your family? What challenges does it present?
- Scan a current newspaper. Note news items that bring change to families. In prayer, read the headlines from the stories. After each one, pray for the families and individuals affected.
- Prayerfully read aloud Psalm 90 or 103. Reflect on God's constant love for a world that is constantly changing. Offer sentence prayers of thanksgiving and praise for God's faithfulness. Sing a hymn that acknowledges the faithfulness of God, such as "Great Is Thy Faithfulness," "For the Beauty of the Earth," or one which you select.
- During this coming week, think of a symbol which could be shared with the covenant group to describe your family. Bring it with you for session ten, and be prepared to explain why you think it symbolizes your family.

10. The Family of God

- ❑ Create a montage celebrating different types of family. Choose a variety of sizes and shapes of boxes. Provide pictures from magazines, scissors, and glue. Each box will be covered on the outside with pictures of families. You might choose to use the inside as well, for private pictures. When finished, the boxes can be arranged as a worship center or other display which focuses on celebrating family.
- ❑ Pray a litany by calling out the cultures, languages, races, ages, countries, ethnic background, and ancestral countries represented in your covenant group or congregation. After each one, say together, "We are God's family."
- ❑ Pray responsively "A Litany for Peace and Children" (p. 79).
- ❑ Sing the hymn "For We Are Strangers No More" (pp. 84-85).
- ❑ If people in your group have traveled, give each person a chance to tell about the family life of Christians in other cities, states, and countries. Pray that we can learn to know them as brothers and sisters in Christ.
- ❑ Share the symbols which you brought to represent your families. Place them with the "box montage" along with other items you wish to include in a worship center. Hand out paper and incorporate your symbol into a family crest or logo. Share your works of art.
- ❑ Close your time together as a covenant group by gathering around that center in a circle, praying aloud for the family of the person on your right until all families have been prayed for. Sing together "Help Us to Help Each Other" or another hymn which your group chooses.

General Sharing and Prayer Resources

Spiritual Espousal

I want to explain more to you about what I
    think this prayer of union is.

You have already heard
    that God espouses souls spiritually.

And even though this comparison may be a coarse one,
   I cannot find another
      that would better explain what I mean
         than the sacrament of marriage.

This spiritual espousal is different in kind
      from marriage;
for in these matters that we are dealing with
   there is never anything
      that is not spiritual.

   For it is all a matter of
      love
   united in love,
and the actions of love are most pure
and extremely delicate and gentle,
that there is no way of explaining them,
   but the Lord knows
how to make them clearly felt.

      Reprinted from *Meditations with Teresa of Avila*, by Camille Campbell.
      Copyright 1985, Bear & Co., Inc., P.O. Box 2860, Santa Fe, NM 87504.
      Used by permission.

Prayer of Intercession

Pray always, and do not lose heart. For the millions of children who are living in poverty, that they might receive the basic necessities to develop their potential,

O God, hear our prayer. Help us not to lose heart.

For the children who cried themselves to sleep last night, stomachs tight with hunger, that they be nourished and comforted,

O God, hear our prayer. Help us not to lose heart.

For the children who will tuck themselves into bed tonight, while their parents burrow into briefcases or newspapers, that families make time to enjoy and celebrate each other,

O God, hear our prayer. Help us not to lose heart.

For the parents who struggle to make ends meet, find jobs, and clothe and feed their families, that they find support and compassion,

O God, hear our prayer. Help us not to lose heart.

For the parents who struggle to make ends meet, find jobs, and clothe and feed their families, that they find support and compassion,

O God, hear our prayer. Help us not to lose heart.

For those in positions of power, that their hearts will not be like that of the unjust judge, but instead be moved by your mercy and justice,

O God, hear our prayer. Help us not to lose heart.

For ourselves, that we are moved from complaisance about poverty and that we find the faithful persistence of the widow to challenge injustice,

O God, hear our prayer. Help us not to lose heart.

"Will not God grant justice to [God's] chosen ones who cry to [God] day and night? Will God delay long in helping them? I tell you, [God] will quickly grant justice to them."

O God, hear our prayer. Help us not to lose heart.

By Shannon P. Daley. Based on Luke 18:1-8. From *Welcome the Child: A Child Advocacy Guide for Churches* by Shannon P. Daley and Kathleen A. Guy. Copyright © 1994 Children's Defense Fund. Used by permission.

Prayer of Confession

Leader: Each day in our nation, when 100,000 children are homeless, living on the street or in shelters,

All: God, we confess that we avert our eyes, and pass by on the other side.

Leader: Each day, when the air is filled with the cries of more than 800 babies born at very low birth weight,

All: God, we confess that we cover our ears, and pass by on the other side.

Leader: Each day, when more than 1,800 neglected or abused children yearn to be hugged,

All: God, we confess that we withhold our touch, and pass by on the other side.

Leader: Each day, when 27 children die from poverty, and 40 die or are wounded by guns,

All: God, we confess that we harden our hearts, and pass by on the other side.

O God, open our eyes, ring in our ears, throw wide our arms, and soften our hearts, that we may receive these

Suggestions for Sharing and Prayer

children in Christ's name, and so receive you who sent Christ. Amen.

Assurance of Pardon

Christ came that we might know ourselves to be God's children. And so we are!

Children of God, believe the Good News: through Jesus Christ we are forgiven.

Amen.

> By Shannon P. Daley. From *Welcome the Child A Child Advocacy Guide for Churches* by Shannon P. Daley and Kathleen A. Guy. Copyright © 1994 Children's Defense Fund. Used by permission.

A Litany for Peace and Children

Leader: As Christians, children ourselves of God, our prayers this day are for children and peace.

People: We pray that our concern for children might grow to include the many children who struggle to secure basic food, shelter, and clothing.

Leader: We pray for the courage to challenge any inequities that deny access to food, clothing, health care, and shelter to our children.

People: We pray for wisdom to guide our families and our nation toward peace, so that the world inherited by our children is as beautiful as the one given to us by God.

Leader: Let us be peacemakers, lovers of God's creation, providing for all children in need.

People: Grant us strength to speak out boldly and with conviction on behalf of children, to the nation and to the world family.

All: For we are called to live as family, striving for peace, justice, and dignity of all; yea, the very kingdom of God on earth as it is in heaven. Amen.

> Adapted from *Who Speaks for the Children?* Used by permission of National Council of Churches of Christ in the U.S.A.

Help Us to Help Each Other
BALERMA CM

1. Help us to help each other, Lord, each other's load to bear, that all may live in true accord, our joys and pains to share.

2. Help us to build each other up, your strength within us prove. Increase our faith, confirm our hope, and fill us with your love.

3. Together make us free indeed — your life within us show, and into you, our living Head, let us in all things grow.

4. Drawn by the magnet of your love we find our hearts made new. Nearer each other let us move, and nearer still to you.

Words: Charles Wesley, Revised *Hymns for Today's Church*, 1982. Words copyright © 1982 by Hope Publishing Co., Carol Stream, IL 60188. All rights reserved. Used by permission.

Music: François H. Barthélémon; adapted by Robert Simpson. *A Selection of Original Sacred Music*, 1833.

Suggestions for Sharing and Prayer 81

O Healing River
Irregular

1. O healing river, send down your waters, send down your waters upon this land. O healing river, send down your waters, and wash the blood from off the sand.

2. This land is parching, this land is burning, no seed is growing in the barren ground. O healing river, send down your waters, O healing river, send your waters down.

3. Let the seed of freedom awake and flourish, let the deep roots nourish, let the tall stalks rise. O healing river, send down your waters, O healing river, from out of the skies.

Text: Anonymous
Music: Traditional hymn melody

When Love Is Found
O WALY WALY LM

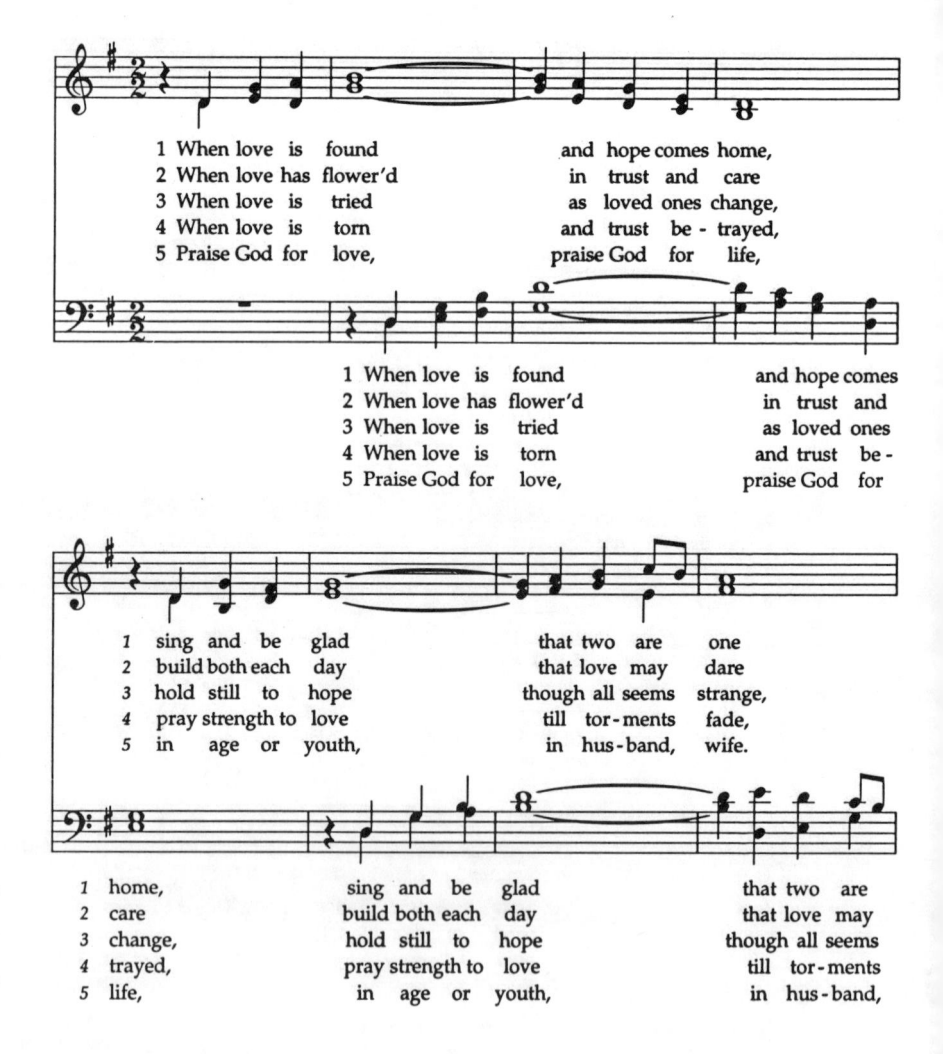

1 When love is found   and hope comes home,
2 When love has flower'd   in trust and care
3 When love is tried   as loved ones change,
4 When love is torn   and trust be-trayed,
5 Praise God for love,   praise God for life,

1 sing and be glad   that two are one
2 build both each day   that love may dare
3 hold still to hope   though all seems strange,
4 pray strength to love   till tor-ments fade,
5 in age or youth,   in hus-band, wife.

1 home,   sing and be glad   that two are
2 care,   build both each day   that love may
3 change, hold still to hope   though all seems
4 trayed, pray strength to love   till tor-ments
5 life,   in age or youth,   in hus-band,

Words: Brian Wren
   Words copyright © 1983 by Hope Publishing Co., Carol Stream, IL 60188. All rights reserved. Used by permission.
Music: Traditional English melody.
   Harmonization copyright © 1989 Alice Parker. Used by permission.

Suggestions for Sharing and Prayer 83

For We Are Strangers No More
STRANGERS NO MORE 11 10 11 10 with refrain

Refrain: For we are strangers no more, but members of one family; strangers no more, but part of one humanity; strangers no more, we're neighbors to each other now; strangers no more, we're sisters and we're brothers now.

Text: Kenneth I. Morse. Copyright © 1979 Church of the Brethren General Board.
Music: Dianne Huffman Morningstar. Copyright © 1979 Dianne Huffman Morningstar.
Used by permission.

Suggestions for Sharing and Prayer

1. Come, walk with me, we'll praise the Lord to-geth-er, as we join song to song and prayer to prayer. Come, take my hand, and we will work to-geth-er by lift-ing all the bur-dens we can share. For we are

2. Where diff-'ring cul-tures meet we'll serve to-geth-er. Where ha-tred rag-es we will strive for peace. Come, take my hand, and we will pray to-geth-er that jus-tice come and strife and war-fare cease.

3. There is a love that binds the world to-geth-er; a love that seeks the last, the lost, the least. One day that love will bring us all to-geth-er in Christ from South and North, from West and East.

Other Covenant Bible Studies available from *faithQuest*

Forming Bible Study Groups
Abundant Living: Wellness from a Biblical Perspective
Covenant People
Disciplines for Spiritual Growth
Ephesians: Reconciled in Christ
1 Corinthians: The Community Struggles
In the Beginning
James: Faith in Action
Jonah: God's Global Reach
The Life of David
The Lord's Prayer
Love and Justice
Many Cultures, One in Christ
Mystery and Glory in John's Gospel
Psalms
Presence and Power
Revelation
Sermon on the Mount